D1470058

GUIDEPOSTS FOR THE SPIRIT:

Stories for Sisters

Guideposts.
FOR THE
Spirit

STORIES FOR
SISTERS

EDITED BY JULIE K. HOGAN

Ideals Publications • Nashville, Tennessee

ISBN 0-8249-4619-7

Published by Ideals Publications
A division of Guideposts
535 Metroplex Drive, Suite 250
Nashville, Tennessee 37211
www.idealsbooks.com

Printed and bound in Italy

Library of Congress CIP data on file

Publisher, Patricia A. Pingry
Associate Publisher, Peggy Schaefer
Series Designer, Eve DeGrie
Book Designer, Marisa Calvin
Copy Editor, Melinda Rathjen
Research Assistants, Mary P. Dunn, Melissa Straw

Paintings by Mary Kay Krell

10 9 8 7 6 5 4 3 2 1

ACKNOWLEDGMENTS
ANDERSON, MARY. "Pillows and Polish." Used by permission of Mary Anderson. ARONS, MARSHA. "Beach
Day" from *Chicken Soup for the Sister's Soul.* Published by Health Communications Inc., copyright © 2002.
Used by permission of the author. BARTOLOMEO, CHRISTINA. "Hunting with My Sisters." Copyright © 1998
by Christina Bartolomeo. Originally appeared in *Glamour.* Used by permission of Dunow & Carlson
Literary Agency. BEDFORD, FAITH ANDREWS. "Sisters Three" from *Country Living,* April 1997. Used by per-
mission of the author. BENNETT, NANCY. "Laughter Among the Soap Suds" from *Christian Science Monitor,*
Feb. 12, 1996. Used by permission of the author. CANTWELL, MARY. An excerpt from *American Girl.*
Copyright © 1992 by Mary Cantwell. Used by permission of Random House, Inc. CHANDLER, MARY.
"Soothing the Sting of Sisterly Squabbles" from *The Christian Science Monitor,* Jan. 23, 1994. Used by per-
mission of the author. CLOONEY, ROSEMARY. "Her Heart on Her Sleeve" from *Girl Singer: An
Autobiography.* Copyright © 1999 by Rosemary Clooney. Used by permission of Doubleday division of
Random House Inc. COUDERT, JO. "My Father's Gift" from *Woman's Day,* June 20, 2000. DELANY, SADIE.
"Sadie and Bessie Delany" from *Having Our Say, The Delany Sisters' First 100 Years* by Sarah and A.
Elizabeth Delany with Amy Hill Hearth. Copyright © 1993 by the authors. Used by permission of Kodansha
America Inc, publisher. DOLAN, JULIE. An excerpt from *Satellite Sisters': UnCommon Senses* by Julie, Liz &
Sheila Dolan and Monica & Lian Dolan. Copyright © 2001 by Satellite Sisters LLC. Used by permission of
Riverhead Books, an imprint of Penguin Group (USA) Inc. *(Acknowledgments continue on page 240.)*

CONTENTS

Shared Histories

I know what's going on. After all, I have sisters too.

LAUGHTER AMONG THE SOAP SUDS

NANCY BENNETT

It was always the girls who washed the dishes. With sleeves rolled up, our foamy arms would soon disappear into the mountains of suds. The warmth of the water, along with the luxury of the bubbles, made us believe that dishwashing was the most enjoyable of chores. It was certainly better than the chores the boys did, and it allowed us a special time of sharing.

The three of us would line up beside the sink and take turns washing, drying, and putting away. We talked about boys at school and compared teachers. We whispered about upcoming birthdays and how we could hint for the items we desired.

We even shared secrets between gleaming white china and two-tone towels. We snapped them at each other when they got wet and often had foam fights with the last of the suds.

Father would call, "What are you guys doing in there?"

We would giggle and say, "Nothing, Dad," as we wiped away the evidence.

Sometimes I would hear Mother giggling softly to herself. She knew what we were up to; after all, she had sisters too.

When I was younger I always wondered why, whenever there was a family dinner, the men got to sit in the fluffy parlor chairs and talk, while the women washed dishes. I thought it was unfair.

But soon, I would hear gales of laughter coming from the kitchen, as my mother and her female relatives spoke in whispers and cracked jokes about the menfolk.

Soon, I was off to the kitchen to sit on a high chair and wear Grandma's apron around my neck as I joined in. Working together in the kitchen until the last pan was shiny and the last bit of news was shared, I felt as though I had joined a secret club, an honored place among my matriarchs. At sinks I have learned about the joyous expectation of a first baby. I have pinky sworn in soapy water with my sister not to tell about her latest heartthrob. I have joked with my mother about her collection of tea bags, left drying on the clothesline by my prankster father.

I have shared recipes and made new friends with women who have picked up a towel and joined in whenever there was a church social or a barnraising. Be it sewing clothes or stitching a wedding quilt for a new bride, the women of my family have always joined in.

At the kitchen sink, on family occasions, four generations of brides, mothers, and new girlfriends will be found sharing and laughing as the last dish of a family feast is put away, to be used again when the next gathering takes place.

My mother bought herself a dishwasher once we had all left the family home. It wasn't so much for the convenience; it was just that doing dishes alone made her sad. I know that whenever we visit, the modern contraption will be set aside for a lingering moment of sharing with her daughters and granddaughters.

Today, I share this chore with my daughters, though if I had sons, I would let them join in as well. My husband's hearty laughter rings through the parlor when it is his turn to wash, and I find myself wondering what bit of gossip he is sharing with our children.

And when it is the girls' turn, I will often hear giggles and the sound of splattering foam or whipping towels.

I will say, "What's going on in there?" and they will answer, "Nothing, Mom!" with twittering voices, trying to control their laughter. And I will quietly smile and giggle to myself. For I know what's going on. After all, I have sisters too.

If we don't help each other, who will?

GET TO THE HEART

BARBARA MANDRELL

After five years of being an only child, I had gotten to like it. I wasn't pampered, but I had loads of relatives and friends fussing over me.

For nearly nine months, Momma and Daddy talked up the notion of how nice it was going to be to have a new baby. I was going to be a big sister, with all the benefits and responsibilities that entailed. People had cared for me, and now when my turn came, I was to care for others. But my parents were not convinced I was seeing it that way.

The baby was born on July 13, 1954, and this time Momma had an easier time with childbirth. A few days later, Daddy brought Momma and the baby home. With me watching, he stormed into the house, shouting: "They gave me the wrong baby. Look at all this black hair. This is not my baby."

With that, Daddy rushed into the bathroom, closed the door, and announced he was going to flush her away. The next sound I heard was the rushing of a couple of gallons of water.

I didn't really believe he would do such a thing, but just in case, I opened the door. And there was the baby, resting in the bathtub. Daddy had just been teasing me. It sounds kind of crude and cruel the way we tell it, but it had the desired effect. From that moment on, she was my baby too.

Years later, I asked him why he did it, and he said, "Oh, I knew what I was going to do. I had it figured out when I got out of the car." There isn't much that Daddy doesn't plan out in advance.

From that moment, Daddy knew that I was part of the team. I was fiercely protective of my sisters, the way my parents had been of me.

They named the baby Thelma Louise, the first name for the aunt who had suffered through my Loretta Young imitations and the second name for a cousin on the McGill side.

We called her by her middle name right away, but to me she was always Sissy. Still is. She was part tomboy and part mystic, a middle child with her own secrets, a woman whose beauty sometimes obscures her music and her feelings.

She was such a pretty baby, with that thick dark hair. It might have given most big sisters a complex, but not me. I did not mind that I thought I was a homely little girl with a Buster Brown haircut and very red hair (which eventually turned blond) even though Louise had this beautiful black hair, blue eyes, pretty features.

I'm not trying to be Miss Modest. If we're sitting around washing our hair and getting ready for a show or something, I can't help noticing that Irlene's hairline is pretty while mine is not. Even with four or five inches of makeup, I still cannot match Louise's eyes and eyebrows.

. . . I don't mind that God made my middle sister the statuesque one. I always tell people, "Well, we didn't have much money, so Momma gave Louise all the vitamins." As for me, I've always wanted to catch a chest cold. I just never had a place to put it. Do I have a complex? Not me.

I claimed Louise as my responsibility. While Momma was making dinner, I had to watch Louise like a hawk or else she would grab a cube of butter off the table and eat it like a hunk of candy.

On January 29, 1956, Ellen Irlene was born. Daddy likes to tell her that he was going to call her Irbalene if she was a girl—sounds like a shampoo to me—or Irbus if she was a boy. To me she was always Ene or Enie. Still is.

We almost lost Irlene when she was less than a year old. We had moved to California, and Daddy was working in security at Edwards Air Force Base. Not long after we got there, Daddy had to swerve his little Volkswagen Beetle to avoid an oncoming truck. Daddy was thrown clear and Momma was knocked unconscious, but Irlene was pinned under the front hood. She was trapped under the car, which rolled over six times, and when the car stopped in a ditch, it was upside down.

Daddy raised the front end by himself and pulled Irlene out. They rushed her to the hospital, where it was discovered she had a brain concussion and a broken leg.

This was the first time my parents had ever left me alone with Louise because they were just going on this short trip home from work. I didn't worry when they didn't come back right away. I made a salad, set the table, and thought it was fun. Then I saw Momma and Daddy getting a ride home with Daddy's uniform all dirty, and I found out they'd had a car wreck.

Fortunately, Irlene recovered. She was just starting to crawl, so they set a cast for her to scoot around the house. Later, they set the cast so she could hold onto a chair and try to walk with it. We used to reassure her that at least the leg healed properly, meaning that one of Irlene's roles is the naive one. But since my own wreck, I don't make jokes about head injuries.

That was just the start of what the family came to call "The Perils of Irlene," after the Saturday-afternoon movie serial thriller *The Perils of Pauline*. She had so many accidents that I used to complain she was only doing it so she could get a present.

"I'm going to jump off the stairs," I would threaten, just so I could get some sympathy too. My two sisters would laugh and say, "You could fall down a mountain and only get a scratch." Those were our roles. I was the formidable one, the leader. They looked up to me. I was rarely hurt. I was indestructible. I never felt any responsibility or pressure to be the leader, I just was. I was the oldest.

The three of us were The Mandrell Sisters as soon as my parents had the good sense to get us all assembled. Our stage was in a trailer or in a series of small houses out in California. We had pets, we put on shows, we played with dolls—all the normal things. We put on Christmas shows and Easter shows and Halloween shows. We wore costumes, sang songs, danced, clowned, did dopey things. Like Judy Garland and Mickey Rooney used to say in all those movies, "Hey, let's do the show right here in the garage." We were doing them in the living room.

Usually with me giving the orders. I loved being a big sister so much that I took charge automatically. I went to their classes; I organized the shows in our living room; I fussed over their clothing and their hair. I included them in whatever I was doing—not to be bossy, I liked to think, but because that was what big sisters do. My parents never treated one of us as special, never tried to divide us.

But I was definitely the leader of the pack. I would give the marching orders to Louise and Irlene [no matter what] was going on. If we were making a dinky little home movie, I'd say, "What can we get Irlene to do?" and maybe suggest that she skip around and look busy. I would organize carol-singing expeditions at Christmastime.

. . . We were always active outdoors, getting into things. One time Irlene was just skipping on the grass when she fell down and broke her arm. The break was so close to the growth control center that they didn't know for forty-eight hours if her arm would grow anymore from the elbow down. They didn't set it, and the arm is still slightly crooked, although nobody can tell except Irlene; and it certainly did not hamper her drumming.

From the moment we were put together on this earth, we became a unit. The Mandrell Sisters. We might quarrel over a game or an item of clothing, but we never had any natural pairings, any two-against-one stuff. I think if Daddy and Momma had caught us taking sides, they would have busted all three of us. Sisters stick together. People would say, "Barbara and the little girls," but that was only because I was older.

Our childhood was a happy blur of homemade cookies and pretty dresses, church and company, little shows we would improvise in the living room, animals all over the place, bandages and bruises, games, and music. I can tell you our childhood was not very different from what we did on television for two seasons. The writers of the show just had to know us for a few weeks and they could fill in the blanks. Or one of us would say, "Hey, remember the time . . . " Whether it happened in Lancaster or Palmdale or El Monte or Oceanside, it worked on television.

Holidays were played out like a ritual supplied by a script writer. We all had our roles. Daddy has always been terrible about having to know what you have bought for him. He cannot wait. One Christmas, I bought him an engraved gold lighter, and I hid it in a shoebox, and wrapped it, and put it in a grocery bag, and put it in a bigger box, which drove him nuts.

Now, I never should have been this stupid, but one day I picked up the phone and a high-pitched voice said, "Hi, what'd you get your daddy for Christmas?" And I said, "a gold lighter," The voice dropped a few octaves and said, "Thank you very much." Nowadays, whenever he wants to tease me, Daddy will say, "What'd you get your daddy for Christmas?"

Mealtimes were for getting together, chattering about what we were doing. Our parents were interested in us no matter how busy they were. . . . Also at dinnertime, when Momma or Daddy was not looking, one of us would take food from our plates and feed it to the latest puppy. Momma said I favored our puppies so much that I didn't eat enough.

One time we found a bird shivering and fluttering in the backyard and we took it inside to our own little veterinary office. I wrapped it up and cuddled it while I was watching television; but after I got up to change the channel, I sat down on the bird and I did not notice it until too late.

I was in hysterics, crying and running out the front door, screaming for Daddy, "Save it! Save it!" but the poor bird died in my hands.

"Murderer!" Louise and Irlene called me. "You killed the bird!"

Now it sounds almost funny, but we were devastated. I'm sure the girls meant it at the time.

From playing with our menagerie, we kind of blundered into the facts of life. There was a rabbit farm down the street. We got one and named it Sammy. Later, we changed the name to Tammy when we found out it was a girl. One day I went to check on the rabbit and I saw all these little creatures swarming all over her. I ran back in and screamed, "These mice are attacking the rabbit!" Surprise. Tammy had been pregnant and we hadn't even known it.

Well, some of us learned the facts of life. After I moved away, the rest of the family moved to Newbern, Tennessee. Irlene would go off into the fields almost every day, carrying a beat-up blue hairbrush.

"Bessie likes me to brush her," Irlene would say.

I thought, "Maybe brushing feels good to the cow." One day when I visited the family, we took a walk into the fields to see Bessie. Irlene was draped over Bessie's back, just brushing away, unperturbed by the large, pointed horns on Bessie's head. Bessie, need it be said, was a bull. You think we made up this stuff about Irlene?

There was always something going on at our house. One Halloween at

Oceanside, Daddy and Momma set up a party in our enclosed patio. We had a record of chains clanking and ghosts howling and the wind blowing. We put the speakers inside the patio, and when kids rang the doorbell, one of us would pull a string, real slowly, and open the door with these eerie sounds coming through. We took turns making frightening sounds into a microphone, and after we had scared people, we would give them candy.

All the kids in the neighborhood started coming around, saying, "We've already been here, but we brought our friends over just to hear this." Irlene and Louise were out trick-or-treating, but they said everybody they met talked about the Mandrell house, so they figured they better come back.

That was how our home was. Other kids were welcome there. I'm not saying we were perfect. We had our squabbles and got our spankings, but there was a feeling that the five of us were a family.

Sometimes I find it impossible to explain to people how close we three girls always have been. I always had this idealistic, fairy-tale belief that all brothers and sisters are so close, and all parents and children are so close.

Yes, in a way the focus was on me, because I had been around the longest. Both girls will say they always thought of me as a big sister who was protective and talented. I was singing in church, and when they were just starting in grade school I was performing in Las Vegas and around California. And even in our hometown, I was chosen Miss Oceanside when I was a sophomore in high school. In most families, jealousy and resentment would be natural, but I didn't feel any of that.

Irlene has said, "I was never jealous. I was always proud. But maybe I was envious. I always thought enviousness was when you were glad somebody had something but you wanted the same thing." I've heard Irlene say it hurt her more than it hurt me if I didn't win one of the major awards from the Country Music Association that year.

Both of my sisters have been loyal and supportive to me. They never complained about my first career as a child performer. In fact, they practiced their instruments so they could join me, the first chance they got. And they have loved and helped raise Matthew and Jaime when I was busy working.

To this day, I depend on my sisters for love and guidance. I talk with Irlene almost every day when I am home in Nashville, and Louise and I share messages on yellow legal pads. We both rely on each other to criticize our shows. If we don't help each other, who will?

Other things may change us,
but we start and end with our family.
–ANTHONY BRANDT

HUNTING WITH MY SISTERS

CHRISTINA BARTOLOMEO

My sister Angela calls me to say she's found her wedding dress. It's from the 1930s. Seven panels of cream satin cut close to the body and pooling around the feet. Long sleeves with wrists that come to a point. A square neckline. She sees it with a Juliet cap and an off-the-face veil.

"What did you pay?" I ask, after weighing the detailed description.

"Fourteen dollars. It's a little stained down the front—tea, I think. But I'm sure it will come out."

And it does. She knew it would, for Angela and I—and our two older sisters—are experts at judging the phoenix potential of a pile of old clothes.

Nor am I surprised that Angela has lined up a wedding dress when she isn't even engaged. She found it at our favorite thrift shop, a true abode of the damned, where the disinfectant they use on the clothes makes your eyes water and your nose run. The racks bulge with faded leotards, abandoned bridesmaid dresses in puce and turquoise taffeta, and ancient fur coats that appear to have been gnawed by packs of bloodhounds. But if you have an eye—ah, the possibilities!

We started training our eyes as teenagers, when our parents sent the four of us, on scholarship, to a private girls' academy. Most of the pupils were the children of wealthy doctors and lawyers; and their clothes, cars, and jewelry shrieked of newness. These girls dressed haute prep school: candy pink polo shirts with lime green pullovers and sturdy, expensive loafers.

Our family could not afford these clothes, and putting up a good front in this shark tank of snobbery was a constant problem. But our mother (who escaped the Boston slums through sheer will and a course at John Powers charm school) taught us early and well how to make do.

Our first heady experiences with hand-me-downs came with the huge cardboard boxes sent by our older cousin Barbara, a pretty and generous debutante from the well-to-do side of my father's family. From one of these hauls came a lemon yellow linen sheath that did good service through my oldest sister's sixth-grade year. (Mary, with her black hair and camellia skin, was the only one of us who could have worn that color.) In the same bundle was a chiffon dance dress with a slip of frothy net. My mother, who had been tutored in simple good taste at the charm school, must have thought it was hideous. My sisters and I thought it was moonlight and orchids and all the romantic things that would come our way when we grew old enough.

"Must you wear that?" said my sister Anna a few years later when I wore new purple corduroy bell-bottoms and a crocheted lavender vest to a matinee of *Godspell* (her present to me for my thirteenth birthday). Following that afternoon of shame, Anna took me in hand, dragging me to thrift shops to search for proper blue jeans. In the process, we discovered older, finer things from the 1920s, '30s and '40s. We began to see possibilities.

These old clothes, these rescued clothes, tell the story of our lives. Anna floated through college in vintage 1950s circle skirts worn with twinsets in baby blue and shell pink, moth holes invisibly darned. In these Debbie Reynolds costumes, she cut a wide swath among the fraternity pledges. For her junior prom Angela wore a pale peach bias-cut nightgown from the 1930s that did full justice to her pinup looks.

The only reason the headmistress didn't banish Angela from the ballroom immediately was that her date was the son of a prominent government official.

For the past ten years or so, my sisters and I have been able to afford department-store clothing. But we still prefer to rummage, preferably together. Even when we are forced to hunt alone, we always return to display our treasures, which we know will be received with empathetic gloating. The last time I visited Angela on the West Coast, she gave me a 1942 cardigan in soft, mellowed cashmere, lavishly embroidered with golden daisies. On the top shelf of my closet is a 1920s evening bag Anna found at the open-air market on Capitol Hill. The bag has daisies embroidered in gold metallic thread—a perfect match for Angela's sweater.

Where does it come from, our love of what is old, well-worn, once cherished? Is it a remnant of our private-school predicament? A search for the kind of past our immigrant family never had in this New World? Or just a deep affection for a good bargain?

Anna tells me, "When we're old, we're going to sit side by side in our rocking chairs at the nursing home and fascinate all the men."

I may not care much about men by then; I suspect that after a lifetime of romantic desires fulfilled or unrequited, I will want the voices of women, the company of my sisters. My hope is that when we are white-haired and fragile, we will get up early on Sunday mornings, dress up, right down to our embroidered pocket handkerchiefs, and sail off in a taxi to the flea market, hunting as enthusiastically as we did when we were young girls.

Be careful of what you ask for, you might just get it.

ALL I EVER WANTED

SUSAN E. JAMES

Why, I pleaded with my mother, did I have to share a room with Linda? I was twelve at the time, and in my mind, at least, my seven-year-old sister was still a child. She went to bed earlier than I did, and the light was turned off at her bedtime. I had to resort to a flashlight under the covers if I wanted to read the latest Nancy Drew mystery.

Secretly, I meditated on the bliss of being an only child with a room all my own. And during that summer, my father seemed to be meditating along the same lines. He was going to night school and wanted a room in which to study quietly, apart from his noisy family. So he decided to build one.

For my father, adding a room to the house was not a matter of calling in a contractor or an architect—it meant getting out hammer and saw, buying some nails, plaster, and lumber, and getting to work.

We children were fascinated with the construction process. My baby brother toddled about the backyard with cries of "hammoah, hammoah" as he dragged behind him a hammer bigger than he was. When the framework went up on the concrete foundation, the room became a forest where we played Robin Hood. When the tar paper went on, it became an Old West saloon where Wyatt Earp and the Clantons stared at one another down the barrels of six-shooters from Woolworth's. When the wiring went in, the metal slugs punched from the outlet boxes were gold nuggets that we miners prospected for in the mountains.

All through the summer the room rose like a miniature magic castle. Daddy built a bookcase into one wall for his schoolbooks, a large closet, and windows facing out in three directions. How I envied him the luxury of a room of his own.

As summer became autumn, work on the room slowed. Around Thanksgiving, there were sudden, freak snow flurries. Southern California is not known for such weather, and in my twelve-year-old memory it had never snowed before. Through the windows of the partly completed room, I watched snow drift from the sky, catch on a net of spider webs strung between the branches of the maple tree, and then spin off toward the ground.

There was something magical about that moment. The room was cold because the heat had not been hooked up yet, and the floor was still bare plywood. But to me the room was the cave of the Mountain King. It was Snow White's castle with snowflakes drifting past the windows. I perched on an old stepladder—the only furniture in the room—and watched the backyard change into a world I had never before seen.

By Christmas, the room was finished—pale blue walls painted, blue curtains shot with gold thread hung, floor laid, heat and electricity turned on.

On the last day before Christmas vacation, I came home from school and found the bedroom I shared with my sister completely rearranged.

"Okay, Linda!" I shouted. "What did you do with my books?"

Linda smiled her smug I-know-something-you-don't-know smile and led me down the hall. My parents were standing in the new room.

"Surprise!" they cried. All my things had been arranged in a new maple bedroom suite. My clothes hung in the closet; my Nancy Drew mysteries lined the built-in bookshelf. I was overwhelmed.

"Daddy knew you needed your own room," my mother said. "So he decided you should have this one."

That night, tucked up in my very own bedroom and staring out the window at the suddenly mysterious and alien backyard in the darkness, I experienced a strange emotion. I was lonely. I had Nancy Drew for company, but I missed my sister's sleepy mumbles. "If you don't turn that flashlight off, I'm telling Mom" had somehow become a missed comfort rather than an annoying threat.

I tiptoed to Linda's room. She was still awake. Together, we tiptoed back to the new room, turned off the lights, and huddled under the covers, giggling. We told each other ghost stories, each begging the other halfway through to stop. Beyond the long windows, moonlight sifted through the branches of the maple tree.

"I'm glad you're back here," Linda said.

I was touched. "Really?"

"Uh-huh. Because now I've finally got a room of my own."

We grew up together. How could we be so different?

SISTERS

MARTHA MASTERS

abel and I were born to the same father and mother, and we both grew up on the outskirts of the same little Texas town. We played with the same dog and the same six or seven cats. We went to the same rural school. And we both attended the same little country church, which was built of brown brick and walnut.

It would seem that with all this sameness, Mabel and I should've been similar in looks and likes.

But we weren't.

I remember Mother scrubbing a squirming, squealing Mabel and telling her, "You should wear a sunbonnet and long sleeves so you don't get so brown. I can't tell whether this is dirt or not."

Frankly, I thought Mabel's skin was pretty. It was glossy and smoothly tan. My own was fair and it freckled in the sun.

But I especially envied her hair, which rippled and gleamed and reminded me of the walnut wood at church. I envied her dark eyes, too, with lashes that matched her thick, long hair.

So, though it hit a sensitive spot, I wasn't really surprised when I overheard someone say, "Martha is personable, but it's Mabel who'll turn out to be the beauty!"

It was true. Mabel was little and cute and knew how to pout prettily and how to flash a dazzling smile—showing teeth that never needed braces (which back then were seldom used)—to reward those who gave her what she wanted. The "person-ableness" that people said I had was mostly pacifism; I'd rather give up than fight for my own way.

But then, after all, as Mother and Dad always told me, "You're older and should set a good example for your sister."

Our far-apart personalities reminded people of the horses on our farm. I was the plow horse, plodding along from day to day. My sister was the palomino, prancing and spirited and an attention-getter.

I was content on our farm. The four of us often picnicked alongside the ponds in our pasture, and Mother topped the red-checkered tablecloth with fried chicken and deviled eggs and chocolate cake. I thought the ponds, which were joined together by thin ditches, resembled tadpoles touching head to tail, swimming across the grassy fields. In winter, I ice-skated from one to another.

Nearby was our barn with wheat bins to play in whether it was winter or summer. No matter how fast I dug caves in the golden piles, the sifting grains swirled into each indentation.

The haymow had a rope swing fastened to the peak twenty feet above and sent tingles down my spine when I mounted piled bales at one end to swoop down and up to the other end.

There were chickens to feed and cows to milk and baby pigs to watch. I thought it a wonderful place to live.

But Mabel always hated the farm. To her, the pasture was "hot" or "cold" or "dusty." The ponds were "muddy." The barn "smelled" and so did the chickens and cows and pigs.

The years passed and I married Tom; the two of us took over the farm because the folks were ready to move into town and "take life a little easier," as Dad said.

Mabel couldn't wait to leave "this old homestead," as she called it. So not long after that, Mother and Dad reluctantly signed an underage consent form for their dark-eyed, dark-haired, vivacious teenager to marry the big-city photographer she'd met while cheerleading for her school.

Her face soon appeared on magazine covers. Her letters, few though they were, first bore Dallas postmarks, then Chicago, New York, and San Francisco.

She was no longer known as "Mabel" but as "Mai Belle."

And she changed her last name as often as she changed the color of her rippling, gleaming hair I'd so admired.

I was aghast at how lightly she tossed aside husband after husband and home after home.

And I was hurt when she told us how she described our farm to her newfound friends. I could just imagine how they visualized the place so dear to me: dust sweeping across the Texas prairies, the windmill vainly creaking while drought-ridden cattle bawled for water, the sagging barn—bowlegged and swaybacked—housing horses that looked the same way. (It wasn't that way at all. She said it just for laughs.)

In fact, I was angry. If she enjoyed her kind of life, that was fine with me, but I resented her making fun of our old home on the farm.

Mai Belle continued her jet-set life even after Dad had died and Mother came to live with Tom and me. I grieved for Mother as I saw her grieving over my sister. Mother looked older each time she said, "I just never raised my little girls that way."

Tom and I cared for Mother. I took her shopping. I gave her manicures and shampooed and set her hair. I ran her errands, and cooked the foods she liked, and Tom attended to her finances.

The years went by, and though we seldom heard from Mai Belle, it seemed her exciting life was waning somewhat. I sensed maybe it was fading for her.

Soon her letters stopped coming.

Tom and Mom and I continued attending church, although the little country structure of brick and walnut had been gutted by fire one winter night and the congregation had built and moved into a new, modern edifice a mile or so closer to the city limits.

For thirty years the three of us prayed for Mai Belle. So did the hometown friends we'd grown up with and whom she'd apparently forgotten.

But for thirty years there was no indication that God had heard our prayers. In fact, I wondered whether he really had. For the last five of those years, we hadn't heard from Mai Belle at all.

We'd stopped looking for letters, when one day the carrier left an unfamiliar envelope in our R.F.D. mailbox at the end of the lane. It was from my sister! "Dear Mother and Martha, I've been thinking how nice it'd be to see you again. It seems I've made a mess of my life and wasted a lot of years. I've let God down and I've let you down too. I don't suppose God wants me anymore and probably you don't either, but I'd like to come home and visit. ("Home?" Was Mai Belle referring to the hated farm as home?) Love, Mabel." (Was Mai Belle back to Mabel?)

Mother was ecstatic. She forgot her arthritic limp and buzzed around the house. Her face and eyes glowed. "We'll get out the sterling and the gold-rimmed china when she comes. In fact, I think I'll give them to her for a coming-home gift!"

"Yes," said Tom. "We'll have to kill the fatted calf."

When he said that I remembered the biblical story of the Prodigal Son, how he'd wasted his life and his money in a faraway land and when he said he was coming home, his father killed the fatted calf to celebrate.

I also recalled the older brother's resentment.

And suddenly I understood how that older brother must have felt. He had a right to be resentful! Maybe that fatted calf had been the one he'd nursed back to health or bottle-fed from birth. Maybe that older brother had stayed home and taken care of the needs and whims of his elderly father. Maybe he'd also re-roofed the barn and replaced worn-out equipment and fixed the fence on the farm without a single thank-you from his fun-seeking brother.

No wonder the older brother was angry.

So was Mai Belle's older sister—furious.

And I was jealous too. Mother planned to give the heirloom china and silver to Mai Belle, not to the daughter who had taken care of her all those years. Mother never hopped around like a twenty-year-old for me; she just related all her aches and pains. Now I had to restrain her from climbing a ladder to wash the windows and trim the hedge.

I didn't know how I'd expected God to answer our prayers, but it wasn't this way!

In a fury I grabbed my Bible and flipped to Luke 15 to re-read the story of the Prodigal Son. How had the brother treated that returning rascal?

I reached the end and sat there, stunned. It didn't say! The footnote simply stated, "This is one of Jesus' unfinished parables."

Unfinished! Did the older brother remain angry? Was he ever reconciled? Did he ever forgive?

How would Jesus have ended the story? I asked myself. And suddenly I knew. The older brother would have said to his father, "Yes, you're right and I'm wrong. I've been self-centered and jealous. I've been acting like a child, not like your son. Please forgive me. Now let me help you make my brother welcome in every way I can."

There was the answer to all my prayers. That was what God was trying to tell me.

I found a pen and paper. I bowed my head for a moment. Then I wrote: "Dearest sister, come on home. Come on home to stay! Love, Martha."

*One's sister is a part of one's essential self,
an eternal presence of one's heart and soul and memory.*
—SUSAN CAHILL

SADIE AND BESSIE DELANY

SARAH DELANY

essie and I have been together since time began, or so it seems. Bessie is my little sister, only she's not so little. She is 101 years old, and I am 103.

People always say they'd like to live to be one hundred, but no one really expects to, except Bessie. She always said she planned to be as old as Moses. And when Bessie says she's going to do something, she does it. Now, I think Moses lived to 120. So I told Bessie that if she lives to 120, then I'll just have to live to 122 so I can take care of her.

Neither one of us ever married and we've lived together most all of our lives, and probably know each other better than any two human beings on this earth. After so long, we are in some ways like one person. She is my right arm. If she were to die first, I'm not sure if I would want to go on living because the reason I am living is to keep her living.

Bessie and I still keep house by ourselves. We still do our shopping and banking. We were in helping professions. Bessie was a dentist and I was a high school teacher, so we're not rich, but we get by. Papa always taught us that with every dollar you earn, the first ten cents goes to the Lord, the second goes in the bank for hard times, and the rest is yours—but you better spend it wisely. Well, it's a good thing we listened because we're living on that hard-time money now, and not doing too badly.

We've buried so many people we've loved; that is the hard part of living this long. Most everyone we know has turned to dust. Well, there must be some reason we're still here. That's why we agreed to do [our] book; it gives us a sense of purpose. If it helps just one person, then it's worth doing. That's what Mama used to say.

Bessie and I have lived in New York for the last seventy-five years, but Raleigh will always be home. Raleigh is where Mama and Papa met as students at Saint Augustine's School, which was a school for Negroes. Mama and Papa got married in the campus chapel back in 1886 and raised all ten of us children right there at good old "Saint Aug's." Papa became vice principal and Mama was the matron, which meant she ran things day-to-day at the school.

I don't remember my mother ever calling my father by his first name, Henry. He was always "Mr. Delany" or "your pa." Now, I do recall that my father would call my mother "Miss Nan" in private moments, but he usually called her Mrs. Delany in front of everyone, including us children. Now, you might think this seems a bit formal. But the reason they did this is that colored people were always called by their first names in that era. It was a way of treating them with less dignity. What Mama and Papa were doing was blocking that. Most people never learned their first names.

In 1918 Papa became the first elected Negro bishop of the Episcopal Church, U.S.A. That's a long way for a man who was born a slave on a Georgia plantation. But if you had known Papa, you wouldn't be surprised. He was always improving himself, and he and Mama brought us up to reach high.

. . . I came into this world at 7:30 in the evening on the nineteenth day of September, 1889. It was a long day of hard labor for Mama. Poor, dear Papa! There wasn't a thing he could do for Mama but worry and pray.

Everyone was nervous because I was Mama's second baby, and the doctor had to be brought in after my older brother, Lemuel, was born two years earlier. This time, Mama wanted her sister, Eliza, by her side. That's why I was born at Lynch's Station, Virginia, where Eliza lived. Mama just got on that old train and headed up there when she was about ready to drop me.

Eliza's presence was calming, and the doctor was not needed. As a matter of fact, after the midwife left, Mama sat up in bed and declared she was hungry! Eliza was just tickled to death at Mama's appetite and cooked up the biggest plate of fried apples and hot biscuits Mama ever saw. Mama said she ate every bite. They named me Sarah Louise, but I have always been called Sadie.

Mama got her confidence back with my birth and went on to have eight more healthy babies. Next in line was Annie Elizabeth, born two years after me and known as Bessie. I don't remember life without Bessie.

"Queen Bess," as Papa used to call her, was born on the third of September, 1891. Like all my younger brothers and sisters, she was born in Raleigh. She arrived at 9:30 in the morning, after keeping poor Mama up all night pacing those pine floorboards, which creaked loud enough to wake the dead. Bessie was so alert at birth that Mama said she had a funny feeling that child would have a mind of her own.

Bessie was what we used to call a "feeling" child; she was sensitive and emotional. She was quick to anger and very outspoken. Now, I was a "mama's child" and followed my Mama around like a shadow. I always did what I was told. I was calm and agreeable. The way I see it, there's room in the world for both me and Bessie. We kind of balance each other out.

Early fame eludes udding-bay ars-stay.

THE PARTON SISTERS

DOLLY PARTON

My sisters were musically abused. That is the only way I can think of to describe what I put them through in my constant search for musical satisfaction. Stella and Cassie were my chief victims. Of course, I was always the star, and I made them sing backup. I would use any kind of promise, threat, or coercion to get them to do what I wanted. "Oh, I'll do your chores if you'll just sing one more verse," or "I'll tell Mama about your boyfriend if you don't sing one more verse," or, "I'll just die and it will be your fault if you don't sing one more verse."

There was one period of time when I just knew I had hit upon a sure-fire formula for instant stardom. I would have my reluctant backup sisters sing in pig Latin. Brenda Lee had not thought of this; what a silly oversight on her part. This was going to be the biggest thing that ever hit radio, TV, or the special live stage that would surely be built so that the entire world could hear us sing, "E-shay, as-way i-may est-bay end-fray." (Translation: She was my best friend.) I had made up all of the parts, and I wanted to hear them. It was of no consequence to me whether my sisters wanted to sing them. It simply had to be done. Even today, if I start into one of our old arrangements, Stella and Cassie will chime in with their parts. I had them so drilled. Somehow pig-Latin backup singing never caused quite the stir I expected it to; we never even made it onto *The Ed Sullivan Show.* Stella and Cassie are probably just as glad that it didn't.

Memories and a brownie camera can capture a lifetime.

IMAGES: SIX SISTERS

ARLENE THORNTON

Five smiling young faces look out from a sepia-tone photo from the 1930s. Five charming sisters, ranging in age from eleven years to twenty-one months, in front of the home we had recently moved into on Hager Street. It is very early spring, Easter, I think, as we pose in like-new dresses with brown stockings wrinkled at the knees, and oxford shoes. This is one of the earliest pictures of me with my sisters.

A few years later two brothers were added to the family and an infant sister, who lived only a few hours. She is remembered like the faintest star in the Pleiades, always with us but never seen. Another baby girl arrived before too long and we were six sisters. A rather impressive number. Mom often referred to us as "her girls" or "her beautiful daughters."

And so we were six, but very different in many respects. We didn't look much alike (redhead, blonde, brunette); we were diverse in personality, talents, style, and demeanor. Many people were surprised to learn we were sisters. Some of us shared school days, playtime, and household chores, but the older ones were already in high school and the others were still too young.

There are not many pictures of all six of us together. Looking through albums I find group images of three or four, sometimes five, but rarely all six of us. One, of the three oldest with bobbed hair and bangs covering their eyebrows, always brings a sigh of consternation. Another memorable image is of a gaggle of girls, taken by our neighbor and good friend, of his four daughters with us five girls in the yard of the house we shared—one family upstairs, one family downstairs.

When our uncle visited with his family, he took snapshots of us with our cousins: on a slide in a park, at a picnic, in front of our house on the porch steps. Another family friend captured family pictures on Mother's Day 1941. All five girls had new Easter coats and hats; our two little brothers, ages two and four, had special outfits. Mom and Dad were beaming proudly.

As teenagers we bought our own brownie cameras and began taking pictures. Rarely were we all in one place at the same time, but there is a lone snapshot of the eight of us—six girls, two boys—when the youngest was about two and a half years old. The first photo of all six sisters (no brothers) was on Mother's Day 1951. By this time our oldest sister was married with children of her own and the youngest had made her first communion. Our favorite aunt is with us in the picture. Other photos included our parents and grandparents; there was even a four-generation picture.

Another family picture was taken around Christmas 1954. We were at our parents' house and a friend framed us in a doorway decorated with Christmas cards and snapped the shutter. It turned out to be the only family picture of the thirteen of us. Shortly after that, one adventurous sister moved away, others married, and our younger brother joined the Navy and died in an automobile accident.

In 1973 our parents had retired and returned to their hometown. We celebrated their fiftieth anniversary. Color photography was in. Long dresses were in vogue. Beautiful family photos were taken that day but still none of the six sisters together.

In 1980, at the wedding of my daughter, the six sisters were reunited and, finally, after fifty years, captured in all their radiant glory. Our festivities were punctuated with childhood memories, and we all agreed that we had waited far too many years for a sisterly portrait. From then on we made an effort to gather and share our special bond at milestone birthdays, our parents' anniversaries, and the weddings of our children, the third generation. Pictures were now more frequent. At a sister's birthday in Denver, we were all wearing similar dressing gowns made by our eldest sister, the seamstress. Another time we were around a table with a birthday cake. In a Chicago motel, five mature bathing beauties lounged in a whirlpool (one must have had an aversion to water that day). There were dinners, celebrations, and family visits when we reminisced and cherished every moment. All with pictures.

Another image is of the sisters again—but different. Our second youngest sister is gone now. She left us much too soon, at age fifty-seven, before we were ready to let her go. Five sisters smiling again at the camera—not the long-familiar brownie camera, but the newest color model.

Later, the five sisters traveled to Ireland—older, wiser, similar in size and shape, some with gray hair, some with wrinkles. It was the "1996 Sisters' Trip to Ireland," the birthplace of our great-grandfather—a trip we hadn't even dared to dream about when we were growing up. Five of us together were experiencing the warmth, the welcome and the beauty of the Irish.

One evening on the western coast, we walked to the shore of Galway Bay and sat on the rocks as we watched the sunset. It was a surreal moment. We sang the song we knew so well, "If you ever go across the sea to Ireland . . . and watch the sun go down on Galway Bay."

Although one sister had gone before us, we knew she was with us. We were six again. We could feel her spirit and almost see her smile and hear her voice.

A
New Sister
Arrives

Sisters are inescapably connected, shaped by the same two parents, the same trove of memory and experience.

—MARY BRUNO

WAIT TILL NEXT YEAR

DORIS KEARNS GOODWIN

My parents had not planned on having me. With two daughters—Charlotte, fourteen, and Jeanne, nine—they thought their family complete. Charlotte later told me she was so embarrassed to discover our mother's pregnancy at the advanced age of thirty-five that she refused to tell her high school friends. On the day I was born, a blustery January day in 1943, my father handed out cigars to his fellow examiners and bankers. One of these colleagues was the father of a high school friend of Charlotte's. When the girl arrived at school the next day and told everyone the news, Charlotte was mortified. Her only hope, she would later tease me, was that I be shut away in the attic until I was grown.

Everything glamorous, comely, elegant, fragrant, remote, feminine, and forbidden was my sister Charlotte for me. She seemed the model of physical perfection: tall and shapely, with high cheekbones, a creamy complexion, large hazel eyes, and long thick hair. She walked with a natural grace and wore a slight smile that seemed to acknowledge her beauty. The star in her high school plays, she thrived on attention and was always conscious of her appearance. During one play she refused to dye her hair gray, fearing it would make her look old at the cast party later that night. I remember her surrounded by adoring boys—one had a Chrysler Highlander with a plush red interior, another a violet Chevy he called the "Purple Passion."

Once, when she was still in high school, Charlotte told us that the new boyfriend she was bringing home had an ugly scar on his right cheek, about which he was acutely self-conscious. She warned us against looking directly at his face when she introduced him. I tried to obey her command, but my eyes were drawn irresistibly to his forbidden right cheek. Seeing no scar, thinking I must have confused right and left, I maneuvered to his other side, which was equally unmarred. Later that night, I asked my sister why she had told us the story of the scar.

"He's so arrogant about his good looks," she replied laughingly, "that I figured it would throw him off if none of you looked at his face."

I liked to sit on a small cushioned stool in the back bedroom my sisters shared and watch them get ready for their dates. Jeanne was shorter than Charlotte by more than half a foot, but she had the same dark hair, thick brows, and large eyes. They shared a dressing table with a fluffy white organdy skirt, arrayed with brushes, combs, tweezers, emery boards, and colognes. I watched in admiring bewilderment as they brushed their hair, fifty strokes at each sitting, and put cold cream on their faces. And I can still see, reflected in the vanity mirror, the expression of discomfort on their faces as they held one eyebrow taut to tweeze imperfect hairs from their perfectly shaped brows. I was something of a tomboy, more comfortable in pants than dresses, with skin that freckled and blistered in the sun. I could not imagine that the day would ever come when I would voluntarily put myself through pain for the sake of beauty.

After Charlotte finished high school, she entered a three-year diploma program at Lenox Hill Hospital in New York to become a registered nurse. She had picked nursing, she liked to say with an ironic turn of her lip, because, "besides saving lives and all that other noble stuff, I'll get to wear a great uniform—all white, freshly starched each day, with long sleeves, French cuffs, and matching stockings." When I was five, I accompanied my family to Charlotte's capping ceremony, which symbolized the end of her six-month probation period and the beginning of the intensive training to become a nurse. Emerging from the train station, I was overwhelmed by the wondrously mingled noises—the sound of police whistles and the multitude of cars rumbling along the streets, and the crowds of shoppers hurrying past the vast and glistening window displays.

The ceremony was beautiful. About sixty student nurses marched in a solemn line toward the stage, lighted candles in hand. The glow from the candles cast a strange and wonderful light on their faces.

"Why are they carrying candles?" I whispered in a loud voice to my mother.

She explained that the candles were in honor of Florence Nightingale, the founder of the nursing profession, who carried a burning light as she tended to the wounded soldiers in a makeshift military hospital during the Crimean War, earning herself the name "Lady with the Lamp." When Charlotte's name was called, she walked to the center of the stage, where she received a white bib with "Miss Kearns" embroidered on top in blue letters, and an organdy cap with a ruffled back that looked like a miniature chef's hat. I was so excited I stood up and cheered, shouting her name as if she had just hit a home run.

The next summer, when I was six, Charlotte took me to Rockefeller Center and Radio City Music Hall. Before we left the house that morning, she used the curling iron on my hair until the strands on both sides curled up evenly. Unfortunately, before we reached the train station, one lock on the right side drooped downward— the same rogue piece that appeared that year in my first grade photo, giving me a page boy on one side and a flip on the other.

Our first stop was Saks Fifth Avenue, where Charlotte planned on buying me a new dress. As we walked up Fifth toward Forty-ninth, the rhythmic click of my sister's alligator shoes on the sidewalk seemed to draw the attention of everybody nearby, even the poodles on their leashes and the mannequins in the store windows. At Saks, she knew exactly what she wanted for me; I had to try on only two dresses to find a light blue one we both loved. From that moment, I valued her opinion on style far more than my own. It was she who taught me not to wear pink with red, not to combine plaids and polka dots, not to wear white past Labor Day. If I didn't always follow the rules, at least Charlotte had made me everlastingly aware of them.

. . . If Charlotte was a distant ideal, living, as she did, away from home through most of my childhood, Jeanne was an everyday presence. For as long as I can remember, she was a surrogate mother, looking out for me, taking care of me when our mother was sick. The nearly ten-year gap in our ages eliminated the potential for competition and defined our roles: she was the grown-up; I was the kid sister. Loving, patient, and gentle, she gave to me more than I gave her in return. Whatever hesitations she must have had about taking responsibility for me, she always made me feel as if she had been waiting for a little sister all her life.

In the summer of 1949, Jeanne was sixteen and about to enter her junior year in high school. She was one of the top students in her class: vice-president of the student organization, treasurer of her Hi-Y club, president of the dramatic club, and leader of a service organization that gathered canned goods for needy families in the Deep South and knitted afghans for veterans' hospitals. Though I had no idea why the people in the Deep South needed food, I got so caught up in the canned-goods drive that, each time I went to the corner store for my mother, I would bring home an extra can of soup and hide it under my bed. When my hidden cans added up to a dozen, I proudly presented them to my sister as my contribution to the overall effort, taking immense pleasure in the thought that my hoarded cans would soon appear on the kitchen table of families far away.

I tagged along with Jeanne everywhere—to the movies, the beach, the houses of her friends. There must have been times when I aggravated her, but she was never openly resentful, and only rarely bossy. On rainy Saturdays, she patiently took me with her to the movies, where she and her girlfriends talked with each other and flirted with the boys. We had two movie theaters in Rockville Centre: the Strand, which had once been a vaudeville house, boasting a live orchestra and a Wurlitzer pipe organ, and the newer Fantasy Theatre, an ornate picture palace designed in an Egyptian motif at the time King Tut's tomb was found, with a deep balcony, lush carpeting, and matrons dressed in black. As long as I kept relatively quiet and curbed my natural tendency to plunge into any conversation—especially when the boys turned the talk to baseball—she let me sit by her side. She remembered that when she had gone to the movies with Charlotte, she was forced to walk several paces behind Charlotte and sit by herself seven rows to the rear of Charlotte's group. No exception was allowed, and Charlotte had warned her that if she told our mother about their arrangements she would be committing a mortal sin in the eyes of the church, called "tattletaling."

The routine continued until Jeanne, in preparation for her First Communion, went to First Confession. She told the priest of her temptation to tell her mother about her unhappiness, though she knew it was a mortal sin to tattle. The priest laughed, and told her she needn't worry. Tattletaling was not a mortal sin. When Jeanne emerged from the confessional with a big smile on her face, Charlotte knew the jig was up. From that day forward, she had to let Jeanne walk beside her on the sidewalk and next to her at the movies.

My sister, in her innocence, was Snow White; and I, in my knowledge, was a wicked Rose Red.

AMERICAN GIRL

Mary Cantwell

The first time I saw Diana, she was wedged into the corner of a wing chair, wearing an undershirt, a diaper, and a belly band over her healing umbilicus. Her fair hair was little more than fuzz, and her scalp was an angry red. But, then, all of Diana was an angry red. She was screaming, her mouth wide open over toothless gums. Perhaps I'd pinched her.

Emilie Connery came around the corner and through the gate many times, box camera in hand, to photograph the Cantwell girls. Each picture is a testament to mayhem. Sometimes Diana is in her playpen, still in a diaper and undershirt and still screaming. I am standing alongside, in what look like lounging pajamas, and my eyebrows are in one long, mean line. Later there are photographs of us with our tricycle. In some of them Diana hoists a plump, triumphant leg over the seat and grins for the camera while I glower. In others I lay a proprietary hand on the handlebars and stare insolently into space. Beside me Diana is screaming.

Our parents dressed us alike, in little smocked dresses and little black patent-leather shoes for Sundays and little overalls and little brown oxfords for weekdays. Both of us had Papa's brown eyes, so we looked a bit alike, but my hair was dark and her hair was light. This made me mad because it meant that I was the evil Rose Red and she was the good Snow White.

Snow White she was, too, dimpled and plump and amiable. But I had thinned out and was all cheekbones and crooked teeth and knees. Esther said that holding me was like holding a bag of bones, and Mother said I'd get into trouble with those hands of mine one day. They were forever after Diana, poking and pushing and, once, going toward her throat until my mother yelled and yanked me away.

Somehow I must have known that once I had no peers, that for eighteen months I had reigned alone. The only time Diana and I were peaceful, when I wasn't shrieking "She did it, she did it!" or "Not fair!" was in bed, in the dark, when I changed her name to Jane and mine to Marie and we conversed. Of what I can scarcely imagine. But I suppose I said things like "Would you like more ice cream, Jane?" and she answered "That would be very nice, Marie."

Other times I tapped out tunes on the maple headboard of my bed. "Baa, baa, black sheep!" Diana would guess, and "Lazy Mary, will you get up!" I liked her then. Even more, I liked not being alone in the dark. I liked the sound of her breathing— she was always asleep before I was—and the companionable creak of the mattress when she tossed and turned.

Diana was a tomboy, tearing her clothes on brambles and suffering scraped knees and playing "Run, sheepie, run" with the Tingley boys until it was too dark to see where anyone was hiding. So it was strange when she started getting the stom- achaches, strange because it was I who complained of cramps in my legs and tingles in my fingers and believed that I breathed through a hole in my throat. I could feel it, truly, the cold air going in and out of the invisible puncture; and for several months, until I came up with a new peculiarity, I had my mother believing it too.

But this was Diana who woke up crying and clutching her belly, so the pain had to be real. Papa and Mother started whispering to each other. Then Mother whis- pered to Ganny and Ganny whispered to Esther, but nobody whispered to Gampa because he couldn't be trusted not to be tearful around Diana, who was his pet and his treasure. Once, when Diana had fallen asleep on the couch, I had watched while he picked her up to put her to bed, and his face was blurry with love.

The doctor who lived up the street bustled into the house often, bringing with him peace and sanity and the reassuring scents of ether and rubbing alcohol, but then he, too, started whispering. Papa, he said, would have to call in somebody from Providence.

The somebody from Providence came down, burly in his topcoat and exuding bonhomie, and said Diana would have to have her appendix out. She cried, fat tears tumbling down fat cheeks, and none of us, not even I, could bear the sight.

Let Papa or Mother even mention the hospital and how she'd have fun and get presents, and tears would well up in those big brown eyes and spill down the cheeks that always had roses in them. "My stomach doesn't really hurt," she'd sob.

The whispering began again, more terrifying than any shout, and I stalked the house with my ears laid flat against my head. Nobody was safe from my ears: Esther said I could hear the grass growing. "We'll tell her we have to take her to Providence for x-rays," Papa whispered to Mother, "and that she'll just have to stay in the hospital overnight. It's the only way we'll ever get that appendix out."

Diana crowed. Neither of us had ever been to Providence, and now she was getting a ride all by herself. Should I tell her what I had overheard? I should not. But now she, in her innocence, was even more of a Snow White; and I, in my knowledge, was even more of a wicked Rose Red.

It was still light on the evening they left for Providence; and Diana, sitting alone in the back seat, her blond pigtails sticking out from under a brown beanie, peered out the rear window at me standing in the roadway. She waved, trustingly and triumphantly, then turned back, safe and happy, to our parents. The car made a left on Union Street, and she was gone.

Two weeks later Diana was home again, with a wonderful scar on her stomach and a wonderful wormlike souvenir floating in a jar of alcohol. It stood on the table between our twin beds, and every day it looked a little worse than it had the day before. Bits and pieces of the worm broke off and the alcohol turned gray and turgid, and every morning I woke up to this disgusting reminder of my necessary crime. But I never begged her to throw it out. Guilt wouldn't let me, guilt and that passion to protect that sooner or later is the curse of the oldest child. Those blond pigtails still recede in the distance, and little wisps of hair still disturb our mother's careful central part.

The position in the family leaves an indelible stamp upon the style of life.
—ALFRED ADLER

WHAT HAVE YOU DONE FOR ME, LATELY?

PAULLINA SIMONS

During an outing to Bear Mountain in New York one September Sunday, I looked at my mother and thought she was wearing a maternity dress.

Now I knew she couldn't be.

One, my mother was thirty-seven years old, and in my thirteen-year-old eyes, practically a pensioner.

Two, a maternity dress would imply that my parents were having s–x, and that certainly wasn't possible.

And three, I was an only child.

"Do you have any brothers or sisters?" people would ask.

"No," I would say. "I'm an only child."

My mother was obviously wearing a loose dress. What did I know about maternity clothes? Yet . . .

Oblivious to my thoughts, my mother continued to stroll arm in arm with a woman friend while my dad and I trailed doggedly behind. The day was sunny and warm. Everybody was quite content.

Everybody but me. My mother's tie-dyed blue cotton dress looked too loose for my liking.

Eventually we returned home to our apartment in Queens, New York, and I went to sleep. The next day I woke up and went to school. I was in ninth grade and was going to be graduating from junior high school at the end of the year. I was soon going to high school, and in three years, I was going to college. I thought of myself as nearly a grown-up.

Grown-ups didn't get brothers and sisters. Children got brothers and sisters. When I was a child growing up in the Soviet Union, I would have given away one of my parents to have a sibling, and, in fact, thought I had when my dad had suddenly disappeared. My mother had told me he was on an extended business trip, but after a year passed, we finally went to visit him, and I saw he wasn't on a business trip. He was in prison for political reasons, I would much later learn. When after two long years he had come back to us, my mother and I saw him only every other weekend for two more years.

Then we came to America and settled in Queens. And now, four years later, out of the blue, my mother was wearing a maternity dress.

My parents were still at work when I came home from school that Monday afternoon. I immediately went through my mother's bureau. Nothing, nothing, nothing. Finally I found a bottle of prescription pills hidden in the back of her makeup drawer. The prescription was in her name. The name of the pills read PRENATAL VITAMINS.

TAKE ONE A DAY, the directions instructed.

Prenatal. What did that mean?

There was no entry under prenatal. I looked up *natal.*

The dictionary said, "Of, relating to, or accompanying birth." It also said, "Of or relating to the time of one's birth."

I read the definition for ten minutes, over and over again.

Just in case, I looked up the prefix *pre-*. "Existing or occurring before," Webster's kindly informed me.

I spent all afternoon trying to wrap my brain around *pre-* and *natal*. I would put the dictionary down, then pick it up again, and look for the word afresh. Maybe I had misspelled it. Maybe I hadn't read the right definition.

At five o'clock, my mother came home, in appropriately tight work clothes. I felt a little better. At six o'clock, my father came home. We ate dinner. Maybe one of them would say something to me. If it were really true, surely they would say something to me instantly.

They said nothing.

I thought, maybe it isn't true.

That night I tried to come to terms with my feelings. They were all over the place, along with my clothes and school papers and books. They were as disorganized as my room. One thing was clear, however. I was an only child. That was my defining characteristic. All my other traits, every one, stemmed from that one. That was the root of my personality, the very core of my identity. I was my mother and father's only daughter, only child. I also knew that my parents were as defined by their one-child-ness as I was. We were a family for fourteen years. A one-child family. Me. I was the child. The one child.

When I had been younger, I wanted a brother or a sister, but then I got older. I still asked for a sibling, but more feebly.

. . . Weeks passed. My parents said nothing to me about the existence of the aforementioned pills. I started weakly hoping I misunderstood the dictionary. Maybe prenatal meant "to prevent natal." Wouldn't that be nice. I was sure that if my mother were actually pregnant, she would have said something by now. I don't know why I thought that. These were my parents we were talking about. When we were leaving the Soviet Union for good, my father told me a mere three weeks before our departure. When I got my period at twelve, my mother somberly stood before me and said that from now on I was going to bleed for about a week every month. Then she walked out and never spoke of it again. My parents never told me anything.

September turned into October, October into November. In November, it got very cold and I turned fourteen. *The Godfather* premiered on television, I had cavities, friends, and a little romance.

Also, my mother's stomach grew.

Her work clothes got looser, her coats got bigger, the robe she wore around the house didn't tie around her waist anymore.

Still, they said nothing. My father came home and we ate dinner. My mother started coming home earlier and taking unprecedented naps in the late afternoon. Sometimes my father would make dinner when he came home. We would eat late on those nights.

My relationship with my mother deteriorated each day. She hardly spoke to me, certainly never kindly. She didn't seem at all happy. Every once in a while, she would leave to go to some mysterious doctor, and I'd be blissfully alone in the house.

In December, my mother no longer fit into her coat and had to buy a new one.

Also in December, we had an ice storm and my father photographed it beautifully, with my ever-enlarging mother underneath a splendid ice-covered tree. In those pictures, no one in the family smiled. My mother and I stood next to each other, making sure the sleeves of our coats didn't touch.

I had given up all illusions and grimly waited.

Finally in January, my father came into my bedroom and sat on the edge of my bed. I was reading. I reluctantly put down my book.

"I want to talk to you," he said.

"Yes?" I didn't want to hear it now. What was the point? Still, I sat up and leaned against the pillows.

Your mother and I—we—all of us—we're expecting a visit from the stork."

"Excuse me?"

"Yes. We're going to have a baby. You're going to have a baby brother." He was smiling out of the corner of his mouth.

"A stork, huh?"

"Yes, a stork."

"I see. When is the stork coming?"

"Sometime in the middle of March." His eyes twinkled.

"And he's bringing a baby brother?"

"Yes, he is."

"I see."

"What? You don't believe me?"

"No."

My father smiled openly. "I'll make you a bet," he said. "If around March twelfth or thirteenth, the stork doesn't knock on your bedroom window and bring you a baby brother, then I will buy you a new pair of shoes."

"Really?" I badly needed a new pair of shoes.

"Yes, really."

"Okay, you got yourself a bet."

He sat there quietly for a few minutes. I could see he was struggling with himself. At last he said haltingly, "Umm . . . do you have any questions?"

Did I have any questions?

Yes. I wanted to know if having a new child meant we would move to a bigger apartment. If my mother would stay home all the time, if I had to baby-sit, and if so, how much they would pay me. I wanted to know if having a new child meant they would never love me again. I stared at him.

"No," I said.

He squeezed my hand hard and left.

In February, during a particularly ugly fight, my mother screamed at me, "I can't believe you're making me this crazy. You know that I'm expecting a child."

That was the only thing she ever said to me about it.

My mother was miserable. She and my dad fought all the time—about nothing and everything. Her huge belly heaving, my mother made veiled threats about leaving all of us. I didn't understand any of it and didn't want to. My concern was mostly for me but partly also for my impending sibling. How was my mother going to give the new baby any affection? She seemed to have none for any of us.

February was cold. I had my own problems. The guy I thought I was going out with asked someone else to our junior prom.

I obsessively listened to Fleetwood Mac's "Landslide" and Carole King's "It's Too Late." I slept badly, lying awake at night, listening to the radio and taping songs.

Already unwelcome changes were upon me. My mother left work; they threw her a big party. That was nice for her, but now she was home all the time. I was not used to having my mother be at home. I thanked God for her long naps.

Our large apartment was apparently too small for a wee infant, so we started contemplating other living options. For now, we moved my parents' bedroom furniture into the living room, which was bigger, and the living room furniture into the bedroom, which was smaller. This did not bode well for the future.

March came.

One Saturday night, March 11, we had Russian pancakes with red caviar and sour cream.

After eating, we cleaned up and sat down in the "living room" to watch TV. It was eleven o'clock at night. Suddenly my mother got up and disappeared into the bathroom. My father went to stand outside the door. I paced in the hall.

Then my mother came out and looked at us—at my father expectantly and at me oddly, as if she was too embarrassed to tell me what was going on.

So she didn't. She just put on her coat. My father procured a bag from somewhere and said to me, smiling, "The stork is coming."

My mother was already heading downstairs.

They left.

I watched TV, I read. Eventually I fell asleep.

At 7:30 in the morning on Sunday, March 12, 1978, the phone rang.

And my definition of myself changed forever.

"I'm coming home," my father said. "You have a sister."

When he returned, he came into my room. I stood up, and my father said, "Plinochka, come here."

He hugged me.

The last time my father hugged me must have been when he came home from prison when I was seven years old.

He said, "Plinochka, you have a sister. We have a little girl. I'm so happy. Your mother desperately wanted a boy, desperately, but not I. No, I don't like boys very much. I much prefer girls, and I'm so very happy."

I patted him gently on the back. It surprised me to hear that my mother desperately wanted anything except to be left alone.

"But I just want you to know," my dad said to me, "that even though we are going to have a new baby in the house, you will always be my favorite, because the way I loved you when you were a baby, I can love no one."

He said all this in Russian, of course. I continued to pat him on the back.

Later that morning, we went to the hospital to visit my mother and the baby.

"What are we calling her?" I asked in the car.

"Elizabeth," my father said. "Leeza. Elizabeth and Paullina. We have daughters right out of Pushkin." Pushkin was the greatest of the Russian poets.

I waited outside on the hospital playground while my father went to see my mother. I swung and swung and swung, quietly singing "Landslide" to myself.

Finally I was allowed up to the fourth floor to see my mother, who was wearing a hospital gown and looked a little pale but was otherwise in surprisingly good spirits. She asked me how I liked the name Elizabeth. I told her I liked it fine. "Your father wanted to name the girl Axinya," she told me.

I did a double take. "You're joking."

"Axinya is a very nice name," my father defended himself. "Axinya. Axyusha for short."

"No," my mother said mock firmly. "We are having an American baby. With an American name. Elizabeth is a beautiful name."

Where is this Elizabeth? I wanted to know.

My mother remained in her room while my father and I walked to the nursery and peered through the hospital glass at cots full of babies.

"There she is!" said my dad, proudly pointing to a swaddled bundle in the middle aisle on the left. "What do you think? She is incredibly beautiful, isn't she?"

She was lying on her side. She was incredibly hairless.

"Look at those cheekbones! Look at those eyes," my father said.

Her face looked round and her eyes were shut.

"She's going to be beautiful like your mother. Thank God she's not going to look like you or me," my father said.

On Tuesday the baby came home.

And my mother came home too.

Tuesday was a good day because my father came to get me out of school early, and everyone in my homeroom knew why. I was cool that day for two reasons. First, there is something special and enviable about being let out of school early. And second, this must have been a first that year—the mother of a fourteen-and-a-half-year-old having a brand new baby. It didn't happen very often. In our school, the fourteen-year-olds—not their moms—were having babies.

We drove to the hospital, and my mother was wheeled out to us. She was holding in her hands a bundle of blankets with no sign of human life inside them. My mother was nervous about the cold weather, but it was actually a sunny, warm March day.

We brought the brand-new baby home and laid her on my parents' bed in the "bedroom." I lay down next to her. I was not invited to pick her up, nor did I offer to. When I lay down next to her, I touched her for the first time. She was soft. My father took some pictures. My mother said, "Stop touching her; you'll wake her up." I stopped and watched her sleep for a while. Then, sure enough, she was awake. My mother and I changed her. We clucked around her, and it was quite something for me to see my mother so unabashedly reverential toward this six-pound squealing bald baby human. "Look at her," my mother said, kissing her. "Isn't she just beautiful? You know, I haven't changed her on my own yet. The nurses helped me in the hospital. I've never used one of these," she said, pulling out a disposable diaper. "We only had cloth diapers when you were little."

Was I ever little? Little like Elizabeth? And did my mother cluck all around me too, kissing me, touching me, stroking every part of me? I found it hard to believe.

The diaper changing seemed to take about four hours. I was exhausted afterward.

I went into the "living room" and turned on the TV. I didn't see my parents for the rest of the day. Actually, I didn't see them again for the next nineteen years.

My life really had changed. They had completely forgotten me.

It was wonderful.

Sometime in April, my father did take me to the shoe store. I picked out a nice pair of shoes for about forty dollars. I was pleased as punch. It was my first pair of shoes in two years and would be the last for another two.

That summer we got our first-ever case of poison ivy and itched uncontrollably—I the worst of all. Elizabeth was miraculously spared, and my parents proudly stated that it was because she was the first U.S. citizen in the family.

Inspired by Elizabeth's spanking-new and attractive nationality, my parents began proceedings for us to become naturalized citizens of the United States. That was one of the things my sister Elizabeth had done for us. She made us all Americans.

Also that summer, we went on our first vacation together as a two-child family. It was the best vacation of my life. My father fished day and night, and my mother sat with my sister outside our little cottage in Perrault Falls, Ontario. I was left to my own teenage devices. A new baby—it was a miracle!

Did I even exist?

Yes, I could tell from the photos. I was the one holding the baby. That was my leg the baby was lying next to. That was my hand propping her up. My hair was in her face. She was sitting smiling against me. I was rocking her carriage. In one photo, I showed the baby her first daffodils.

"She is the most beautiful baby in the whole world," my father proclaimed, and for once I did not disagree; but I harkened back to that Sunday in March when he hugged me and told me I was always going to be his favorite. I realized he had just been trying to make me feel better because he knew how upset I had been.

I had been upset once upon a time, but that was before Elizabeth was born. Yes, she was beautiful, and thank God they were busy staring at her and didn't notice what time I would come home.

Though once, they noticed. One warm spring night, instead of baby-sitting, I went to my girlfriend's house. My mother, who never called me at my baby-sitting jobs, called the only time I wasn't there. My parents were frantic for four hours, until I finally strolled in at midnight. Understandably, there was a big to-do. I thought, they care; they still care. I was so touched. I actually apologized to my mother for not calling her and letting her know where I was. Apology-wise, I think that was a first.

Later that night, when we were sitting in the living room, as my mother held the sleeping Elizabeth in her arms, she quietly spoke to me. "Once when you were a baby, you got sick—with scarlet fever or pneumonia, I can't remember now. You had a raging fever. . . . I was up all night in a chair by your bed, listening to you breathe."

I thought, did you hold the sleeping me in your arms, too, Mom, as you now hold Leeza? I couldn't speak.

I needn't have worried about my mother; she lavished, drowned my sister with affection. My mother could not take her hands off that baby.

Incredibly, a backwash, an undertow of that love flowed to me. That's another miracle my sister Elizabeth performed, She let my mother touch me again.

For the first year and a half of Elizabeth's life, my mother stayed home. That was odd and strangely unpleasant. I had been a latch-key kid, always alone after school. Now suddenly in the middle of a perfectly nice afternoon, there was my mother, full of conversation just when I wanted to eat and read my book.

Then in the summer of my sixteenth year, my mother decided to go back to work and leave me with the baby. I wanted to be out with my friends, but there was nothing I could do. My mother paid me a dollar an hour, and I had to put away my low-quality, only-child traits—my selfishness, my self-indulgence, my vanity—and become an older sister. It was then that I learned how to take care of a human being. I never had time for myself anymore. There was drool and food, and worse, on my shirts. I had to keep my hair unattractively back so Elizabeth wouldn't pull on it. I had to take her for walks, and what could be better for cramping teenage style than having your classmates see you with a toddler? But in the process, with soiled clothes and ugly hair and exasperation stamped on my forehead, I learned how to become a human being. That was what Elizabeth had done for me.

Later that same summer, my grandparents emigrated from Russia, and we all moved to the suburbs. We needed a bigger place to fit my baby sister, so we built a house and my beloved grandma and grandpa lived in it, too, and took care of Elizabeth while my mom and dad worked. Because of Elizabeth, we had our own house for the first time in our lives. Because of Elizabeth, my mother and father's American dream came true.

I graduated from high school when I was seventeen and left for college.

Then I went to England and then to Kansas and then got married young and had my own daughter young. And I knew just what to do with her, astonishingly. Because I had been given a sister late in my adolescence.

Once when I was briefly back home, I observed Elizabeth horsing around with my mom, who was tickling her. My dad was standing nearby, and suddenly he started tickling her too; and then the three of them just hugged and held on as I stood and watched. Elizabeth was thirteen at the time. I was twenty-seven. And I thought, I'd never had that kind of moment with my parents. That's what she had done for them. As she did for me, she helped them become human beings too.

And now I have a twenty-year-old sister. She is the latest thing in cool. She has a tongue ring and pink hair and hangs out with kids just like her. She is studying art in a New York City college and has changed apartments four times in the last year. At first she lived in a hotel room next to a woman who used to urinate in the public shower. Thank goodness, she doesn't live there anymore. Every once in a while, I send her care packages full of macaroni and cheese, Oodles of Noodles, Pop-Tarts, cereal, and double-chocolate Milanos. "Paullina," Elizabeth says to me on receiving the package, "You told me you were sending me Milanos, but there aren't any Milanos."

"I know. I ate them all," I say. "Next time."

She grunts.

"Leeza," I tell her, "You're my favorite sister."

"Paullina," she says, in a long-suffering tone of someone who's said this a thousand times before, "I'm your only sister."

If I had to do my life over again, I would have preferred a sibling when I was small, when it would have done me the most good. And for Elizabeth too—I wish she hadn't been alone after I left for college. I wish she and I could have been spared the one-child loneliness, though to Elizabeth's advantage, she has had me and lifelong friends and a home she has lived in most of her life—three things I had not had.

My sister and I aren't close together in age. Still, we have each other for life.

My sister recognized that the more blessings she could invoke, the longer my mother would stick around before saying good night.

PRAYING FOR MOTHER TO STAY

JOHN GOULD

somewhat delicate situation developed during my fetchin'-up, and I've long wondered if it should be given more thought. I was the firstborn of four. And as my introduction to piety, and all the other good things, my mother taught me a short child's prayer. She'd had it as a girl from her Scots mother, and she in turn from hers, in a heritage that went back to the first mother of the Hebrides. It has kept everybody honorable. We have all paid our taxes on time, have never gone afoul of any laws to speak of, have never run for public office, and we eat brown eggs. We've been good people. Probably the wee prayer at Mother's knee has been influential. It is also a prelude to wonderment:

Gentle Jesus, meek and mild, look upon this little child.
Pity my simplicity, and suffer me to come to Thee.

Then, before I was to say "amen," I could add my personal beatitudes, and I would say, "God bless Mummy and Daddy, my grampies and grammies, Uncle Bije and Aunt Nora, all the poor people," and anybody else I might want to include, except that I left it there and that was it. It was my sister who saw the possibilities and developed the blessings into a major production.

She was three years younger than I, so in due time she was caused to memorize the same prayer. From our adjacent bed and crib, she and I would supplicate together under Mother's devout direction before Mother closed the door and went downstairs to the living room where she spent the evening knitting, sewing, darning, and tatting while the house was so quiet.

The moment of evening prayer was routine. We got our jammies on, with concomitant delay and amusement, and Mother was the best person to have around for such ceremonial activity. Then came the prayer and a few proper words from Mother about being a good little boy and a good little girl. Then we'd get a real clapper of a love-pat to make us smart, and we'd be tucked in. We got a kiss on our foreheads and the covers arranged, and it was good night, sleep tight!

When my sister was big enough, she said her extra words about blessing folks. Once, after she had taken care of Mum and Dad, the various uncles and aunts, cousins and grandfolks, she added, "and God bless Mr. Prout . . . "

Mother said, "Whoa! Who's Mr. Prout?" My sister said, "You know Mr. Prout!" My mother said, "I think not. Who is he?"

I believe, if you wish to give this some thought, you'll be inclined to feel, as my mother did, that meeting an unknown gentleman unexpectedly in the coziness of your daughter's prayer is cause for inquiry. So you will not be surprised that my mother pressed the issue. Mr. Prout, my sister explained, was the man from the gas company.

At that time, we were piped for city gas, and we had a meter in the cellar. The meter took twenty-five cent pieces only, and when we had used a quarter's worth of gas, the meter shut off the supply until we put in another quarter. Mother would put a cake in the oven and say, "There! Now my quarter'll run out before it's baked!" And when my father cleaned out his small-change pocket, he'd put the quarters in Mother's gas cup on the kitchen shelf.

Mr. Prout came once a month to go down to our cellar and take Mother's gas quarters from the meter. And although Mother said nothing to indicate it at the time, I sensed, small as I was, that she hadn't expected to find Mr. Prout in my sister's prayers. But in thinking it all over, you'll agree that Mr. Prout came into this beneficence in logical fashion and nobody should be astonished.

My sister recognized that the more blessings she could invoke, the longer my mother would stick around before saying good night, and Mother was a good one to keep hanging around as long as you could. Thus began, in my sister's precocious mind, a deliberate plan to delay our mother's departure by padding the list of benedictions. I never timed her, but I think she ran over twenty minutes the night she included the members of Congress, one by one.

My mother, never duped by excuses to delay bedtime, did indulge Sister in these requests. Only when there were guests to play whist, or she was working on a difficult bluebird on a hooked rug, would she butt in and say, "All right, Skookins, knock it off. You'll have the angels up all night as it is!"

One evening, my sister besought a blessing on Jimmie Morton, the red-headed boy in the corner house who had a brown puppy and chewed bubble gum. My mother said, "Who?" My sister said, "You know Jimmy." My mother said she didn't seem to place him: "Which corner does he live on?" My sister said, "Oh, any corner. I made him up." It was part of Sister's strategy to keep Mother with us a few more seconds, and after that for quite a few years I kept wondering what did get blessed and what didn't.

Mother accepted Jimmie Morton and would ask my sister how he was doing in school and if the pup was growing, and she'd say, "If I ever catch either of you chewing any of that bubble gum like Jimmie Morton, I'll skin you out with a dull knife, I will!" So we never did, and she never had to, and one evening my sister said we didn't need to pray anymore about Jimmie Morton—he'd kicked the bubble gum stuff. Mother said, "You see how it is?"

From the very beginning it was clear she would be a source of excitement and challenge.

LOVE CAN BUILD A BRIDGE

NAOMI JUDD

he final spoke in the family wheel came when I was six: Margaret Victoria was the last of Glen and Polly Judd's children. I remember with clarity the day they brought her home. The six of us slept in the same room for a long time. From the very beginning it was clear she would be a source of excitement and challenge. There was healthy friction between us as she grew older, the type of competition that can only exist between two siblings cut from the same cloth. She was always streaking around with her grubby, noisy little friends and showering an inexhaustible amount of energy on all of us. Margaret was a genuine nuisance to me as I self-consciously strove toward adolescence. Still, I was glad to have a sister. I saw a lot of myself in her from the beginning, and we would eventually become very close, during a crucial period in our adult lives.

Surviving the awkward trials of being a budding teenager was sometimes made even harder by the irritating presence of a pesky little sister. When I began to date, she'd bolt for the door, throw it open, and proudly inform the poor unsuspecting boy that I was still in my housecoat and big pink curlers. She'd describe with glee how ugly I was without makeup and how long I spent in the bathroom getting ready. Now, don't get me wrong, Margaret was a heart stealer. With her soft blond curls and beautiful face, she was angelic looking. Everyone commented on how well behaved she was. Still, none of this stopped me from nicknaming her "Maggot."

Lessons from My Sister

By slight indications the sisters could convey much to each other.

–E. M. FORESTER, FROM *HOWARDS END*

BEACH DAY

MARSHA ARONS

When I told my three older children that we were going to have a new baby, each had a different reaction. Anny, the oldest, at twelve, promptly burst into tears. She had never been good at handling change and was always the child who needed the five-minute warning when we had to change activities. I think she also cried because, though she couldn't express it, she was at that stage where she had just learned what one had to do to get babies and was mortally embarrassed that her friends would know that her parents still did "that!"

Rachael, three years younger and wanting something different than just girls in the family, promptly announced that she would call the baby "Jacob." It didn't matter that the baby turned out to be a fourth daughter. Rachael called her sister "Jacob" and took every opportunity to dress her in blue until Elliana was four months old.

Kayla, four at the time, promptly announced that when the baby came, she herself would give up her pacifier so she could be one of the "big" sisters. She did.

It wasn't until several years later that I realized how profoundly and distinctly each older sister had imprinted this little one, and I guess, each other as well.

A few weeks before Anny was to leave for college, I took the four girls to the beach. With twelve years between the oldest and youngest child, it was getting nearly impossible to find an activity that we could all enjoy together. At eighteen and fifteen respectively, Anny and Rachael often (and understandably) didn't want to do things that were appropriate and fun for their eleven- and six-year-old sisters. More often than not, these older two, who had grown quite close since the previous fall when Rachael entered high school, were off on their own with their own friends.

But going to the beach was one activity we could all enjoy together. Summer was almost over and everyone was feeling the approaching strain when Anny would leave for college. Already, it seemed a hole in the fabric of our family was looming. The girls didn't talk about it outright, but I knew each of them could feel it. I did too.

The sun was high and hot as we unloaded our gear and slathered on sunscreen. But the breeze off Lake Michigan was cool and the water looked inviting. I set up a big umbrella, spread out the blanket, and prepared to park myself under it to read. The three older girls went down to the water's edge to look for shells and get their toes wet. Elliana settled down next to me with a shovel and pail and proceeded to build a sand castle. After a few minutes, she asked if she could go down to the water with her sisters.

Unwilling to relinquish my comfortable position, I called to the big girls and motioned for them to come back. I asked them if they would watch Elli down by the water and let her gather some shells. To my surprise, they agreed without an argument.

I watched them walk away from me—four tan, perfect little bodies in various stages of growth: two womanly shapes with long legs and slim hips; one still with baby fat around her middle carefully hidden under her older sister's oversized T-shirt; and one still in the sweetness of little girlhood, tiny, pudgy, deliciously unself-conscious.

They held hands.

I went back to my book for a few moments, secure that I could trust the older ones to make sure Elli did not venture too far out in the water. But then something made me put my book down and look for them.

They were walking down the beach, the two older ones in front, Kayla next, Elli trailing behind. Every so often, one of them would call to the others, bend down, pick up some found treasure, and put it in Elli's pail. Then the little procession would continue. But I noticed that Elli was not looking for shells. She was playing a different game, watching her sisters. She seemed to be hopping from side to side, following directly behind them. When they stopped, she stopped. Sometimes the older three walked with each other, side by side. But Elli always stayed behind them.

It took me a few minutes. Then I realized what she was doing. Elli was walking in her sisters' footprints.

The afternoon wore on. We ate and napped under the big umbrella, the girls using each other as pillows. When it was time to go, I gathered everything up and we loaded the car. I waited until we were all in the car to ask Elli about her game.

She told me, "I was trying to walk in only Anny's prints. But she takes too big of steps, so I had to use Rachael's feet or Kayla's to get to Anny's. It didn't matter whose footprint I was in, but I wasn't allowed to step on the sand outside a print. That was the game."

Her sisters heard her but they didn't pay too much attention. Or so I thought. Several days later when I was helping Anny pack the last of her things before she left for school, she said, "I wish you hadn't had me first."

I thought she was expressing her fear at leaving home so I started to reassure her that everything would be okay, that she would love college. But she stopped me.

"I'm not nervous about going to school. I'm nervous about not being everything they need me to be."

I hadn't realized how seriously Anny had taken her responsibility as the oldest sister. She knew, had probably known all along, how much they looked up to her.

I wanted to tell her that she had done her job, had given them what they needed when they needed it, that she was a good role model. That each of them would make decisions in life influenced by each other but always lead by her good example. She was a good big sister, the best big sister. I wanted to tell her all that.

"The other day at the beach . . ." she began.

It was my turn to stop her. I said, "The other day at the beach when you were in the lead and the others followed you? When you set the pace, always looking back to make sure they were right behind you where they were supposed to be? When I didn't get up once—not once—to check on any of them because I knew you were watching out for their safety as you always do? That day at the beach?"

I smiled at her, knowing better than to cry.

"Do you think they'll be okay without me? They can miss me a little, but do you think they'll be okay? You know, Rachael has done some things this year in high school. . . . I promised her I wouldn't tell."

"Then don't," I said. "Evidently, you handled it."

"But she's the oldest sister here now." She stopped and thought a minute. Then she said, "Let them call me whenever they want, okay? Don't ask them why, just let them. Promise?"

I promised, aware that we were talking about some secret sister bond that existed among them completely apart from me.

I hoped my oldest daughter would realize that as they had done that day at the beach, each sister would follow in the footsteps of one of the others. But, as Elli had shown us all, it was always available to hop from one sister's prints to those of another, if needed. Because each sister, influenced by the others, would leave her own indelible mark in the sand—and on the world.

She got it. Among the socks and underwear (and her sister's sweater, probably unbeknownst to her sister), that were going off to college with Anny were four tiny pink seashells, carefully wrapped up in tissue paper.

Just a small memento from a day at the beach.

I knew from that day that we were remarkably alike.

BORDERLINE

KATHLEEN NORRIS

Dear Kathy,

I feel hurt because you wrote a book and I didn't. Happy for you and I try read your book and I was bored with it. Mom and dad and everybody talking about it. I feel left out but it will pass. Hope you understand how I feel about your book. I telling you how I feel and I starting to cry while I write this letter.

This comment on my book *Dakota,* which became a surprise bestseller in 1993, is by far the best response I received. It bored my sister Becky. Not for the first time in our relationship, she became a kind of *amma* for me, a desert mother challenging my complacency, allowing me to see the world (and myself) in a new light. By calling me back to the important things in life, my sister seemed as wise and stern as Amma Syncletica, a desert monastic of fourth-century Egypt, who said that "It is impossible for us to be surrounded by worldly honor and at the same time to bear heavenly fruit." Syncletica sums up, I believe, the difficulty writers have in America in surviving success: to keep bearing fruit one must keep returning, humbly, to the blank page, to the uncertainty of the writing process, and not pay much heed to the "noted author" the world wants you to be. Becky's letter was a godsend—reading it over, I found myself released from much of the tension induced by sudden notoriety, the rigors of a book tour stretched out over two years; too much travel, too much literary hoohah.

Becky's life has been a kind of desert. When she was born, the doctors at Bethesda Naval Hospital gave my mother too strong a dose of anesthesia. Having already given birth to two children, she knew something was wrong when she couldn't push enough to release the baby from the birth canal. Precious oxygen was lost. My mother recalls one doctor saying to another, "You got yourself into this mess; let's see you get yourself out." While the doctors squabbled, my sister's brain was irreversibly damaged.

Becky is diagnosed as "borderline." She is intelligent enough to comprehend what happened to her when she was born. She is not intelligent enough to learn mathematical computation. A tutor my parents hired when Becky was in third grade told us that Becky could grasp a concept long enough to work out several problems in the course of an hour-long session, but that by the next week she'd have forgotten what she'd learned and have to start all over. Her teachers had been passing her along; there were no special education programs then, and no one knew what to do with her, or where she belonged. Becky's life has been lonely in ways that most of us could not comprehend.

Yet our family ties are strong, and for years we've acted as Becky's advocates within the educational and medical establishment, sometimes taking consolation in the fact that Becky is a good enough judge of human nature to wrap psychiatrists round her little finger. Several times, when she's been given a tranquilizer or some other drug she didn't like, she's learned enough about the contraindications to fabricate symptoms so that the doctor would be forced to change her prescription. When she realized that alcoholic families were fashionable—or at least "in" with therapists—she convinced one psychologist that her mother was an alcoholic. (My mother is the sort of person who, on a big night out, might order a bit of bit of crème de menthe.) In order to survive in her desert, my sister has often resorted to being a con artist: you get what you want by telling people what they want to hear.

She learned all of this, of course, in the bosom of our family. Our parents decided when Becky was very young that she didn't belong in an institution, but with us. I believe that being raised with myself and a brother, both older, and one younger sister was good for Becky. I know being raised with Becky was good for me. Very early on, I had to learn to respect her intelligence, although it was very different from mine. I also came to respect her tenacity. When she was two years old, and learning to walk was still beyond her capabilities, she became adept at scooting around the house, always with a security blanket in hand. I also had to learn to discern the difference between what Becky was truly incapable of knowing, and what she was simply trying to get by with. When she destroyed my first lipstick by writing with it on a brick wall, I took off after her. She yelled, "You can't hit me, I'm retarded." She learned that she was wrong.

When I was in high school, I began to discover how much my sister and I had in common. We were both in difficult situations—I was a shy, ungainly newcomer at a prep school where many of the students had been together since kindergarten, and Becky had a particularly unsympathetic teacher. On coming home from school, she'd immediately go to her room and play mindless rock music—"Monster Mash" is one that I recall—while she danced around the room (and sometimes on her bed). She talked to herself, incessantly and loudly. The family accepted all this as something Becky needed to do.

One day, as Becky carried on her usual "conversations," with her teacher, with other girls in her class, with a boy who'd made fun of her, I was doing homework in the room next door and realized that I, too, needed release from daily tensions, a way to daydream through the failed encounters and make them come out right. Usually I lost myself in reading or practicing the flute, but sometimes I listened to music—Joan Baez, the Beach Boys, Bob Dylan, Frank Sinatra, Verdi overtures—and imagined great careers for myself, great travels, great loves. I didn't have the nerve to stomp around my room and yell as my sister was doing, but our needs were the same.

We were both struggling with our otherness, although I did not know it then. Now that I'm a writer, it's clear to me. Rejection comes to everyone, of course, but for those who are markedly different from their peers, it is a daily reminder of that difference. To most people, my sister and I didn't seem to have much in common, but I knew from that day on that we were remarkably alike. If nothing else, this insight helped me to survive the intensely competitive atmosphere of my prep school. I knew that getting a D on a math test was not the worst thing in the world. And when I got an A-plus in English, when my writing won praise from my teachers, I could put it in perspective. I knew there were other kinds of intelligence that were just as valuable, needs that could not be satisfied in school.

Our parents are nearing eighty years of age, and while they often seem to have more energy as the years go by, the fact of their mortality looms large for their children. Becky, God bless her, is incapable of hiding her fears. We went for a walk one Christmas Eve not long ago, and she said, out of the blue: "I don't want Mom and Dad to die. I worry about what will happen to me."

"It scares me too," I replied. "But *everyone* is scared to think about their parents dying." I'm not sure I convinced Becky on that score—she tends to think that she's alone in her suffering, and all too often in her life, that has been the case. But I believe I did manage to reassure her that her brother and sisters would not abandon her.

As we walked through a light Manoa Valley rain—bright sunlight, prickles of moisture on bare skin—I remembered the two little girls who used to hide in their rooms every afternoon after school. How good it is to have those difficult years behind us. Becky will tell you that she's "slow." I guess I've always been fast by comparison. What does it matter, on the borderline? We're middle-aged women now, and our parents are old. As for the future, human maturity being what it is, the slow process of the heart's awakening, I sometimes wonder if Becky is better equipped for it than I.

*My own childish behavior and my sister's goodness
taught me a valuable lesson.*

SISTERS AND LADYBUGS

Lauren Zylberman

It was the summer I seriously began thinking about the ladybugs. There wasn't much else to do, anyway, besides lie on the beach and watch those little red dots. I mean, there was the lake and all. But Lake Michigan wasn't the warmest lake. And I always got cold easily.

So I'd wander down to where the water met the sand and watch the ladybugs. There were hundreds of them, thousands maybe—all of them scurrying here or there—and I wondered if they ever knew where they were headed. Sometimes the ladybugs would fight. It was really funny the way they rolled on top of one another. A mass of molten lava on the golden sand. A pile of cherries on a layer of pie crust. Then they'd spread apart, and at least ten ladybugs would be left on their backs, struggling to turn over. Legs up in the air, waving, trying hard to get somebody's attention.

Sometimes I'd feel sorry for the ladybugs and turn them over myself. But I liked it better when I'd leave them there. I liked that because the others always came back and there was that pile of cherries on the sand again. This time, when they'd spread apart, not one ladybug would be left on her back.

My friend Tatum and her mother came up to South Haven, Michigan, with my family every year. Tatum was my age. Sam, my sister, never left us alone. She could not understand that being three years older, we were way too cool to hang out with her. It was the same every summer. But this year it was bad. Really bad.

I remember one afternoon in particular. My mom was not happy with my insistence on leaving Sam out of our beach plans. The outcome of the argument was predictable; Sam became the caboose as Tatum and I set off for the beach. I wouldn't even look at her.

We were about halfway there when Sam realized she had forgotten to put sunscreen on her back. "Tatum," she asked, "can you put lotion on my back?"

"Don't do it, Tatum," I said. Tatum looked at me as if she were the helpless subject of a ruthless tyrant. Then at Sam. "No, I can't, Sam," she said. I smiled.

I will never forget Sam's eyes when she saw that smile. And I will never forget the stab I felt in my stomach at that moment, though I just looked away and pretended it wasn't there.

We got to the beach and Sam wanted somebody to go into the water with her. "The water's warm today," she said in a quiet voice. Her voice bothered me. So I guess on that day I didn't like warm water. Tatum might have wanted to go in. But she didn't want to cross me. So Sam went in alone.

I watched the ladybugs. A couple were on their backs. I thought about helping. But I didn't feel much like doing that.

After a long while, Sam ran up to us. "It hurts!" she cried. Then she turned around. Tatum screamed. I looked up at Sam's back. I'd never seen such a brilliant red in all my life. Not even in one of my old crayon boxes.

Tatum threw a towel around Sam and helped her toward the condo. I followed, feeling the knife dig a little deeper into my stomach now. I began to wonder what Mom would say. I began to wonder if ladybugs got sunburned.

When we went in, Mom ran to Sam, knelt beside her and asked her why, oh, why did she never listen when she was told to put on sunscreen? How many times would it take until she learned? And Sam looked at me with watery eyes and said,

"I don't know, Mom. I'm really sorry. I must have forgotten." And so the knife went in even deeper.

Sam couldn't be in the sun for a while. She had to lie in bed with wet rags on her back all day long. And Tatum didn't want to hang out anymore.

So I went to the beach by myself one day. I sat under an umbrella and watched the ladybugs. Not even one was struggling on her back. That's when I saw that we aren't so different—the ladybugs and us. Sometimes a ladybug needs to fall on her back for the others to notice. Sometimes she needs to be on her back for a while, to make the others see that they can't leave her that way.

I walked back to our condo and went to the sink. I grabbed a washcloth and ran it under the cool water. Then I went into Sam's room. She was lying on her stomach, asleep. Her back was looking better now, it really was. As I pressed the cloth to her back, gently, so as not to wake her up, I felt the knife leave my stomach at last. And I promised myself that I would be there when she did wake up. That I'd be there for her, always. I really would.

A strong connection with your sister is a comfort.

ANIMAL CRACKER DRESSES

CRICKET HARDIN VAUTHIER

I never thought having a sister was particularly enjoyable until I grew up and realized how much more annoying people who aren't related to you can be. My sister, Lori, was born four years after I was, which in kid years is the difference between two lifetimes. Growing up, I had already seen it, done it, and figured it out by the time my little sister got around to it, therefore I was omnipotent and she, well, wasn't.

I wanted a buddy, like a girl version of *The Hardy Boys.* (Shawn Cassidy was my first crush.) Instead, my buddy smelled like peanut butter and was prone to running around the house sporting a bumper sticker—only a bumper sticker. I wanted someone more dignified for my adventures. My buddy created adventures rather than helped solve them. Case in point, it was first grade, and it had taken all year for my turn to take the class hamster home for the weekend. Guess who freed Fluffy at six A.M. Saturday morning? None other than my three-year-old sister who proclaimed to a sleeping household, "De wat got out!" The adventure came in the form of my mother chasing Fluffy around the house with a tennis racket.

Payback came a year later when I persuaded Lori to take a candy cane from the supermarket, unbeknownst to my mother. Once in the car, the evil truth surfaced— my mother had raised a four-year-old thief. Back into the store they marched, clutching the now sticky candy cane. I got to wait in the car. My sister did not reveal until years later the identity of her accomplice.

I was very aware of our age difference since it usually meant I was allowed to do more grown-up things like stay up late or ride the scarier rides at the fair. Lori, however, never saw an age difference and was forever attempting to copy everything I did. This was irritating because I was much too sophisticated to be emulated by a child.

When you are ten, fashion discoveries occur frequently. I thought I had found a new way to wear my hair that was sure to catch on in photo shoots around the world—the side ponytail. Never mind that in 1979, someone was bound to have done this type of thing before. There I was, sporting my new hairdo for all to admire and the only person who even acknowledged my true fashion greatness was my sister, who was more than willing to follow the trend. This became the standard for the rest of my great discoveries: miniskirts, U2, Nicholas Cage in the classic movie *Valley Girl*, and so on. She was perfectly willing to give me credit on these, which strengthened our relationship and my confidence.

Best that I can tell, sisters come in two categories: ones who look alike and ones who don't. Lori and I don't. People often commented on our lack of resemblance; she has dark hair, skin, and eyes, while I am very fair. Our mother once dressed us in matching red and blue animal crackers dresses for our annual picture at Sears. That was the only day when I heard the "Oh, you two must be sisters" comment. To this day I inspect her for something that I can recognize as mine and say, "See we do have the same elbows!"

In spite of our opposing looks, we happen to have the same voice. Hers is capable of singing, mine is most assuredly not, but otherwise identical. This was an instrument of torture for my boyfriends in high school through college. Often there would be the prerequisite quiz at the beginning of every conversation, "What color jacket did Mr. Peters wear today in economics?" "Aha! Mr. Peters teaches trigonometry, put your sister on!" To this day when I leave a message on voicemail for my husband, and I call later to check my messages, it takes me a minute to realize it's me and not Lori telling my husband I am running late.

My sister and I have this thing where we will send our mother the same birthday, Mother's Day, or Christmas card without knowing, despite living a thousand miles apart. We also tend to call her or each other at the same time even though we are in separate time zones. I don't feel it if she burns her hand on a hot stove, nor are there any plans to start our own Psychic Sisters Network anytime soon, but it is comforting to have a strong connection with my sister. We have started collaborating on cards before we send them to ensure our mother gets a well-deserved variety.

Sisters teach you many things, and mine is no different. The most important thing I learned from Lori is how special our relationship is. I hit her once during one of our "You wore my shirt" brawls, and the look that came across her face was not one of pain, but of betrayal and devastation. I had crossed the line and become a bully rather than a role model and trusted ally. The regret I felt that day provided me with a clarity in which I saw the full meaning of our relationship. Lori had always grasped the importance of our friendship; I did not understand it until that day. I gave her the somewhat stretched shirt as an apology. She accepted and we never fought again . . . that day.

We shared a room until I was ten. When nights became spooky, we shared a bed as well. We shared bowls of dessert, until I spit chocolate pudding back in the bowl. Ultimately we shared a lifetime. Our mother taught us to love each other and reminded us daily that each of us is the only sister the other would ever have. I have learned that she is the only sister I could ever want.

Shining
Moments

*Having a sister is like having a best friend you can't
get rid of. You know whatever you do, they'll still be there.*

—AMY LI

THE RACE

DANIELLE GOLDSTEIN

A single pink balloon wafts into the thin air above Boulder as thousands of women of all shapes and sizes prepare for a three-day journey to Denver. On the stage, a survivor explains what it means to have courage in the face of death. Down below, participants summon their own courage to face the sixty-mile walk ahead. When it is time to go, the women in pink shirts are allowed to go first. It is their right, or their luck, or their fate that has allowed them to be part of this powerful event. Hand in hand the women file out of the stadium down an aisle created by hundreds of onlookers—friends and families, husbands and sons, grandmothers and daughters—clapping, yelling, and cheering each woman on to her own special victory.

Somewhere near the back of the mass of walkers, another drama is taking place. It is a small drama, but a significant one, especially if you have a sister.

"Darn it! I lost my bandanna."

"Do you have the car keys?" my sister yells from a crouched position. Her twelve-dollar socks are bunching in the toe of her shoe. Scores of women file past on their way to the love tunnel. *This is not a race. This is not a race.* I repeat the phrase until finally my sister stands up, adjusts her fanny pack, and repeats, "Do you have the car keys?"

Six months earlier my sister pitched the idea of participating in a three-day walk to benefit breast cancer patients and research. She broke her back the January before, and as part of the healing process, she wanted to train for an athletic event. Besides, she reasoned, it would be a great way for us to spend time together without the added dynamic of kids and husbands. And, best of all, we could pool our fundraising resources to quickly come up with the nearly four thousand dollars needed to participate.

Hmmm. Memory, Aeschylus said, is the mother of all wisdom. And conscience, I reasoned, is the grandfather of all decisions. I did not immediately commit to my sister's request. For two weeks I examined my conscience and summoned key memories. Chief among my concerns was motivation. Why did I want to do this? Thus, the selfless-selfish paradigm was born. On one hand, my sister and I agreed it would be great to get outside ourselves, to do something for other people. We, thankfully, did not know anyone with breast cancer. I imagined what it would be like to join over two thousand women in such a worthy fight. As a teacher, I was no stranger to altruism. On the other hand, there was something in this for me. Just think of the admiration and respect I'd win from donors and cancer patients alike. I have to admit, in the recesses of my mind I also wondered if participating in this event could somehow safeguard my sister and me from such misfortune.

I also thought about all of the times my sister and I had undertaken physical challenges and how each collaboration had ended in disaster, or at least dirty name-calling and threats of bodily harm. Like that high school doubles tennis match in 1988 when she swore at me for double faulting, causing us to lose the second set five to seven. I still remember her frosted mauve lipstick as she mouthed the sailor-like words at me. Or the time I served and hit her in the back of the head. It was an accident. I swear.

Hmmm. Would I be wise to undertake this monumental event with my sister? What would be different this time? Who's to say we wouldn't end up tripping each other on a training walk only to sabotage the whole event? What would prevent us from succumbing to the annoyance only sisters can evoke and stomping off the event path into the mountains never to be seen again? Should I choose to undertake a stressful, difficult event with my sister?

"Yes, I'll do it." The die was cast. "But," I added, "there will be some ground rules."

The teacher in me shone. I e-mailed my sister a spreadsheet listing every living relative, friend, and acquaintance. Next to each name was the initial of the person responsible for contacting and soliciting a donation from the lucky victim. Unsure about her follow-through, I included a draft of my fundraising letter, a bullet-pointed list of fundraising strategies, and a five-month timeline. My plan was foolproof.

Three months later, she had raised three hundred dollars. According to my calculations, I was on track, having raised exactly seventy-five percent of my goal. I was so impressed with myself, I didn't let my sister's lackluster report unnerve me. I encouraged her to be aggressive and gave her the name of the event hotline and the website address of a fundraising guru.

"I'm just trying to concentrate on the training," she said. "This week I did the two-and-a-half-mile loop around the pond with the baby jogger."

Two thousand miles away, my training regime was well underway. Early on a hot Saturday morning, I almost killed the neighbors' dog in an overzealous attempt to log fifteen city miles. We had to stop at a café to cool the dog's paws in a bowl of ice. Shortly after, the dog plopped herself down on the lush grass of a funeral home and refused to budge. We had to call for emergency backup.

Meanwhile, my sister and I talked on the phone every other day. The topic du jour was always blister prevention. I recounted the special trip I took to Boston to purchase the walking shoes suggested by the event literature. She countered with tales of jaunts to the premier women's athletic apparel store on Pearl Street in Boulder. There she was able to purchase a non-chaffing sports bra and shorts. Did such a thing exist? We wondered if we should buy another pair of new shoes before the event, just in case.

My sister remedied our fundraising woes with a last-minute solicitation to our father who graciously made up the difference. I had a feeling the list I provided ended up in the bottom of the diaper bag. For the rest of the summer, our spirits ran high. In mid-July, just three weeks before the event, we converged in Wisconsin at our parents' house to spend our vacation preparing for the main event.

Training for a sixty-mile walk is a lot like watching paint dry. Training for a sixty-mile walk on the flat, blacktopped roads of Wisconsin in July is a lot like hell. Your hands swell and your feet burn. If you're lucky, the killdeer won't chase you or swoop at your head. If you're unlucky, you'll have to squat behind scraggy cornstalks and hope the farmer is nowhere in sight. If it's a good day, your Camelback canteen and sixty-four-ounce Gatorade will last, and you'll make it home only to sit twitching in a sweaty pile on the tile floor in front of the TV for the rest of the day.

In one of our shining moments, my sister was convinced we were about to be attacked by a semi driver who pulled over just after he passed us. I suggested he was simply visiting the cornstalks. She was unconvinced and panicked. Armed with sticks and stones, we bravely marched past the truck straight toward Lake Michigan. We rewarded ourselves with a Coke from McDonald's five miles up the road.

Because I had spent so much money on walking accessories, I decided to drive to Colorado with my sister and her two toddlers to save money. After three days and too many roadside diaper changes, we finally arrived. Twenty-four hours later, we were standing in line outside UC-Boulder, waiting to get our tent assignment and event pass.

Everywhere women were wearing T-shirts printed with the faces of loved ones they'd lost to breast cancer. We hadn't even watched the motivational video, and already we were passing our only tissue back and forth. I was surprised at how young so many of the women were when they died. For the first time we understood that we, too, could lose each other that way.

Waiting in line at a dozen check-in stations that day I began to look at breasts in a whole different way. Some women had them, some didn't. According to the T-shirts of a team of women from Iowa, there are over one hundred ways to say breasts, Spanish words included. How strange that this feature of a woman's anatomy had united all of these passionate, courageous women in one place. I thanked my sister for giving me this experience.

On day one shortly after we were ushered through the love tunnel and onto the streets of Boulder, my sister and I caught up with her training group. More accurately, the group of sixty-something grandmothers caught up with us. *It's not a race. It's not a race.* There are two ways to tackle a twenty-mile walk, and slow and steady never wins the race, I thought. The important thing was that I was with my sister. I kept telling myself that.

At the first pit stop, I felt an adrenaline surge when, from my place in the port-a-potty line, I spotted my high-school rival speed walking into mile three with her super-coifed friend. My sister told me she would be there, but I had put it out of my mind. That night at the mobile tent city, I ducked behind a group of walkers in the towel tent to avoid her glance.

We camped in a sea of little blue tents. Two by two, tired walkers hobbled and limped their way around camp. The evening's festivities included group stretching and blister patching. Both were cut short when a nasty storm pushed in over the flatirons. For two hours we lay listening to the rain. When we couldn't stand the drip-dripping anymore, we donned our plastic rain ponchos, strapped our spelunking lights around our heads, and set off for the port-a-potties once again. It was *Revenge of the Nerds* meets *Night of the Living Dead*. My sister said I looked like an alien under the mix of light and rain. She reminded me that we could see her in-laws' house from our tent as we sloshed through the mud in the middle of the night.

On day two, we were no longer talking. An early-morning argument over coffee and pancakes led us to go our separate ways. My newly acquired East Coast pace and sharp tongue got the best of me. I told my sister she was too slow and that I might as well crawl. Hurt and offended, she left me for a new-age girl with beads around her neck and smart rock climbing shorts of an undetermined lightweight fabric.

I spent the day trying to catch up to my high-school rival. First she took my spot on the tennis team, then she stole my boyfriend, and now she was going to win the race.

By the end of the day, I missed my sister. I wondered how her back was holding up. I worried that she had been one of the eleven people that day to collapse of heat exhaustion. Perhaps she had given in and ridden the air-conditioned party bus to the next mobile tent city. I was soaking my feet in a bucket of ice water at camp when I saw my red-faced sister stroll in. She had a spring in her step and a smile on her face. She pulled up a folding chair and found a bucket. When we realized how many walkers had used those same buckets to soak their open blisters, we died laughing.

That night my old high-school friend-turned-rival joined us at the long table in the food tent. We hadn't spoken in years. After three hours of catching up, I remembered why I had befriended her as a teenager. Even after three successive pregnancies, she hadn't lost her sense of humor or zest for life. We made plans to walk into Mile High stadium together.

My sister got stuck in the shower line on morning three and my high-school friend walked off without us, but I wasn't upset. I packed our gear and helped our neighbors fold up their little blue tent. We were among the last walkers out of camp, but I didn't care anymore. With renewed vigor we walked through the streets of Denver. People sat on their porch steps and cheered us on. For the last five miles, we caught up with my sister's training group. A hefty woman at the head of the line led Army chants, and we forgot how much our feet ached.

We spotted the stadium on the horizon. A new friend took our picture in the parking lot of a gas station with our destination in the background. I quickened the pace and my sister obliged, but two blocks from the entrance she insisted on stopping at Burger King. We took another picture with our giant drinks and enjoyed a few minutes of air conditioning. By the time we finally reached the stadium and were herded inside and up the elevator to the holding room, my high-school friend was waiting at the top with the coveted event T-shirt. She and her big-haired friend cheered and clapped with two thousand other women. I couldn't fight the tears. I wedged my way to the front and joined my friend and sister to greet the last walkers. Together we followed the women in pink T-shirts and paraded into the stadium for the closing ceremony.

On the way we spotted our husbands with my nephews hoisted high onto their shoulders. They looked confused and amazed and happy to see us. We cried again, and with a mixture of fatigue and joy, we listened to another survivor tell us what it means to have hope in the midst of a life-threatening disease. Dark clouds threatened to cut our celebration short, so I held my sister's hand and hugged my old friend goodbye. We wound our way through the throng of walkers to our weary husbands. I tried to savor the feeling of accomplishment and wonder.

Studying our blistered, swollen, sun-poisoned legs, my sister's three-year-old said, "What happened to your other legs?" My sister smiled and we wondered what else had changed during the past three days.

Sisters, naptime, and mischief are universal.
—CATHARINE PONDER

PILLOWS AND POLISH

MARY ANDERSON AND LIZ LUCAS

My three-year-old sister and I, who was four, were with a baby sitter while Mom went out to her meeting. When she returned, she asked, "Well, how did it go?" The sitter was happy to inform her, "Wonderful. They slept all afternoon."

"Now that's unusual," Mother said. And then she cried, "Oh, oh!" as she dropped her purse and raced up the stairs to our room.

We weren't sleeping; we had heard her come in. Our dirty deeds were soon to be discovered, but we hurried to hide the evidence.

After we found Mom's nail polish, it had been such fun to paint whatever we could, and we were proud of our artistry. Then after taking our short nap, we discovered that feathers came out of our pillows. We proceeded to pull and pull. The more we pulled, the bigger the hole in the pillows became, and we soon had a pile of feathers mixed with and stuck to the nail polish artwork.

When we had heard Mom come in the front door, we knew we were in trouble but thought we could hide it all from her. We took the pillows to the closet where the window was open, unlatched the screen, and threw the pillows out. The wind caught them and whipped them around causing more feathers to spill out. We watched spellbound and soon, like snowflakes in the middle of summer, the whole neighborhood could see our impish handiwork.

What counted was the people, not the plans.

A SUMMER STORM

PAULA SPENCER

I had been looking forward to my sister Patti's visit for weeks. I had the whole thing planned. It would be one of our usual action-packed, short-but-sweet get-togethers: a nice meal, a little Scrabble, some shopping, an outing with our kids.

When Patti arrived, lunch was simmering on the stove, a new one-dish pork recipe. A carrot cake that I'd actually made from scratch was in the oven. Everything was perfect. Then, a few minutes later, a terrific clap of thunder rattled the windows. A storm had galloped in out of nowhere.

And just as quickly, the lights went out—for the next twelve hours.

It seemed like disaster. Our long-awaited plans! My homemade lunch! We tried to remain hopeful. We'd just eat late, that's all. And the mall was open till nine, anyway. But as minutes turned into an hour, and then another, I had to give the kids cereal. We grownups wistfully eyed the unfinished pork and nibbled on peanut butter sandwiches.

"Now what?" we all wondered.

As Patti and I battled our disappointment, the children battled restlessness. "What? No TV?"

"The TV isn't working," I explained.

So they begged, "Well, how about a video, then?" "Can't you just microwave some popcorn?" I quickly realized just how much we all took electricity for granted.

As the evening wore on, I also realized that I had been taking something else for granted: the power of relationships. The point of my sister's visit was not so we could spend money at the Old Navy store. It didn't matter if we took our kids to the zoo or, as it turned out, showed them how to make shadow bunnies and pterodactyls with their hands on the living room walls. What counted was the people, not the plans.

We all carry the fantasy of perfect get-togethers in our heads. Planning and anticipating such events can be fun, but it's important to know where the imagery stops and the reality starts. Become too attached to your idea of how something is supposed to be, and you'll spoil your chance to enjoy what's right there in front of you.

We wound up singing old camp songs and putting on shadow plays. After the kids eagerly went to bed with their own flashlights, Patti and I brought kitchen chairs onto my small front porch. At first we lamented how all our plans had been ruined. It's hard to let go, after all. Then we sat back silently, listening to the rain dripping through the trees.

I hadn't sat out there in ages, and the night air felt blessedly cool. Time seemed to move more slowly, just as it had earlier that afternoon when we were singing endless verses of "Old MacDonald" with the children. It was strangely soothing to focus on each other, with no TV, no Scrabble board, no malls or sale signs to distract us.

We began to talk about mutual friends. We planned our parents' upcoming anniversary party. Soon we were reminiscing. "Remember the time lightning hit our house while Mom was upstairs packing for vacation?" "Remember how we played detectives all summer at the lake?" Our conversation went places it hadn't gone in years.

I realized that what Patti and I had been looking forward to most was each other—something that often seemed obscured on past whirlwind visits. Those other hectic get-togethers have always been enjoyable, but I must admit that they tend to meld together in my memory. That night the lights went out, on the other hand, will burn brightly for a long time.

Mother's tradition creates a lasting bond among sisters.

SISTERS THREE

FAITH ANDREWS BEDFORD

When Mother died, Dad gave up the summer house. "Come and take what you want, girls," he had said to us. And we did. I chose the tall secretary where Mother sat so often writing letters by a sunny window. Beth chose a painting of the summer house. Ellen picked a statue of horses, for she and Mother had shared a love of riding. Then we put drawers full of old letters, slides, and faded photos—the collective memory of a family—into a dozen boxes, and each of us chose four.

Later I sat on the top step of my porch and opened a box marked "albums." Here were photographs of my father, resplendent in his Navy uniform, and one of my mother leaning against their first car. As I leafed through the pages, the family grew. We bought our first house; the cars got bigger. Then, on the last page, there was a picture of us in our matching "sister dresses."

I could almost feel the starched ruffles and hear the rustle of the crinolines that were needed to keep the skirts full. I remembered Mother's delight when she found these outfits at the children's shop in the village. There was one in my size and one for Ellen, but no size four for Beth. We were so excited when the shopkeeper told us she could order a dress for Beth that would come in time for Easter.

When the box arrived, we gathered around Mother as she lifted out the dresses. They were made of clouds of swiss-white organdy with blue flocked dots. The skirts and collars were trimmed with tiny blue bows. "To match your eyes," Mother said.

We were allowed to try them on just once so we could have a fashion show for Father that evening. As we twirled into the dining room in our finery, he burst into applause. We daintily grasped the ruffled skirts and executed our best curtsies.

As I looked at the photograph, I could recall the warmth of the pale spring sunshine on our faces on Easter Sunday. We must have resisted putting on coats to go to church. They surely would have crushed our dresses, and besides, how then could anyone have seen how beautifully we matched?

In time, I handed my dress down to Ellen and she handed hers down to Beth. But those dotted swiss creations were only the beginning of a long parade of matching sister outfits. I remember the year of the blue calicoes and the year we all had yellow jumpers. Even Father got into the spirit when he came back from a business trip to Arizona with Mexican dresses for each of his girls—including Mother.

Those wonderful white dresses, with rows of bright ribbons edging the wide collars and hems, had skirts that were cut in a complete circle. Father put Ravel's "Bolero" on the record player and we spun madly about the living room, our beribboned skirts fluttering like butterflies. At last we crashed, giggling, into a heap. Dad sat in his armchair and grinned his that's-my-girls smile.

I remember these first sister dresses so clearly that I'm surprised I can't remember the last ones. Maybe Mother knew we were outgrowing the idea. I think she saw how different we were becoming and just stopped buying us matching dresses.

By the time we were adults, our lives were on three very distinct tracks. Mother would shake her head in bewilderment and say to Father, "How did we get three daughters so different?" He would merely smile.

We knew Christmas would be bittersweet that first year without Mother. For as long as I can remember, Dad had always given Mother a beautiful nightgown at Christmas—long and silky with plenty of lace. The tree sparkled, but there was no big box from "Sweet Dreams" beneath it. Though we put on happy faces for the sake of our children, the little touches that Mother always added were missing.

Suddenly Ellen drew out from behind the tree three identical white packages. On the lids, written in Dad's bold hand, were the words "From the Nightie Gnome." We opened the presents, revealing three identical red flannel nightshirts.

Whooping with delight, we pulled them from the tissue paper and ran down the hall to put them on. When we came back to show off our sister-nighties, Dad had put "Bolero" on the stereo. We joined hands and did an impromptu dance. As the music grew louder, we twirled around faster and faster, ignoring the widening eyes of our disbelieving husbands and the gaping mouths of our children.

I smile now at the sight we must have made: three grown women dressed in red flannel nighties whirling madly through a jumble of empty boxes and wrapping paper. When the music ended in a clash of cymbals, we crashed, giggling, into a heap.

Our husbands shook their heads in wonder. The younger children nearly keeled over with embarrassment while the older ones held their sides with laughter. Dad just cracked his that's-my-girls grin.

Mother never realized what tradition she'd started.

*Is solace anywhere more comforting than
that in the arms of a sister?*

—ALICE WALKER

SOOTHING THE STING OF
SISTERLY SQUABBLES

MARY CHANDLER

y sister, newly married and still in her lacy pale pink wedding dress, kneels beside one of the open packing boxes in her new home.

"I know it's here somewhere," she says, stirring through the keepsakes of a lifetime. She sighs. "You can't imagine how nice it is to have space for all my treasures."

I nod, remembering the cramped house where she lived during her first marriage.

"George and I even have an attic," Kaye says.

She smiles and her deep-brown eyes sparkle, just as they did years ago, when she was ten and I was fourteen.

Kaye and I shared a chilly upstairs room in a house built by our father. The bedroom next to ours belonged to our brothers and was strictly off limits. My Saturday morning job was to clean our bedroom, and I hated it. I was tidy; she was a slob.

∽✦∽

"Come here, Kaye." I would say as I all but dragged her into our dressing room. "Look at your clothes!"

Dresses, skirts, and blouses dangled askew on the rod, each one hung by Kaye shoving the hanger through a buttonhole.

"So?" she asked.

"So, why do you have to be such a slob? I've shown you a million times how to hang up your clothes."

I jerked everything off the hangers and threw it all in a heap on the floor. "Now do it right, or I'm telling."

I grabbed the dust mop and pulled it across the old hardwood floor, past the dresser and under Kaye's bed. Along with the usual dust balls, out came orange and banana peels, dried bread crusts, comic books, socks and underwear, and an assortment of little kids' toys.

Without saying a word, I dumped everything except the underwear into two brown paper bags. Through the window, I saw flames leaping from the incinerator. I smiled and raced down the stairs.

"Stop! Please stop! I promise I won't do it again."

I heard Kaye's footsteps and ran faster. I was on a mission.

"No! No!" she cried, as I dumped everything into the flames. As she reached to retrieve her treasures, the soaring fire singed her long auburn pigtails. Tears streamed down her face, and she sat down in the dirt, sobbing.

My mother reached Kaye, gathered her into her arms, and chastised me for tormenting my little sister.

"Why do I have to share a room with her?" I asked. "Why can't she clean it? I hate her!"

That afternoon, my friend Carie came to visit. I shut the door so Kaye couldn't come in, and we sat down on my bed. Carie was lucky. She had her own room. She listened to my complaints, without saying a word.

"Are you finished?" Carie asked. I nodded, feeling smug and self-righteous.

"I've always wanted a sister," Carie said. "Kaye's not that bad. Maybe you just need to give her a chance to grow up."

"I'm moving into the attic," Kaye told me two days later.

I smirked. "I thought you were scared of mice and spiders."

"I'm not that scared. Besides, Mama said she'd help me clean it."

That afternoon my father secured a plywood partition along the unfinished attic wall and moved Kaye's bed into that dark, cramped place. When I got home from my piano lesson, all my sister's personal belongings were out of my bedroom. "Want to see my room?" Kaye smiled and took my hand.

On the door hung her Campfire Girl's necklace, plus stickers, drawings, and school projects, all arranged in a pattern.

"Come in," she said, opening the door. She reached up, grabbed the long ceiling cord, and switched on the bare bulb. Her comic books were in a neat pile on the floor, right beside her bed. School books rested in open boxes. A large paper sack stood in the middle of the room. I smelled orange peels. Two drawers held what wouldn't fit elsewhere. A warped dresser mirror was perched in the corner.

"I won't be bothering you anymore," she said, "except to get my clothes." Those huge brown eyes looked into mine. "And I promise to hang up my clothes right." She threw her arms around my neck. "You can come and visit me any time you want," she said, "'cause you're my big sister and I love you."

My stomach tightened. Tears stung my eyes. I wanted to tell her that I loved her, too, but the words stuck in my throat.

❧❧

"Speaking of attics, Kaye," I say, "remember when you moved into the attic at home?"

Kaye laughs. "I sure do. I liked having a private place where I could play with my friends."

"Everything you owned, you crammed in there."

"Yup."

"But it was so small."

She chuckles. "So was I." She begins to shuffle through the next box.

I shake my head. "Kaye, you stayed in that attic for over a year."

"So?"

I touch her arm. "I guess what I'm trying to say is that I'm sorry. Can you forgive me?"

"For what?"

"For being so unkind."

"Goodness, that was a long time ago, Mary." Kaye smiles. "Don't worry about it!"

I wipe my eyes. "Did you find what you were looking for?" I ask, as Kaye holds up a lavender vase.

"No," she says, shaking her head, "not yet." Those gentle brown eyes look into mine. "Did you?"

I wrap my arms around my sister and hug her hard. "Yes," I whisper.

*Sometimes you have to grow up before
you can become sister-friends.*

–AUTHOR UNKNOWN

A TOUCH ON THE SHOULDER

HAVEN WEBSTER

Two winters ago my stepsister, Dana, came to live with us. She was my age, fifteen. Her dad is my stepdad, and he lives with Mom and me and my younger sister, Heidi, in a small town just south of Greensboro, North Carolina. Dana and her brother had lived with their mom in a nearby town. My stepsiblings had spent weekends with us for years, and I had always enjoyed having an extra brother and sister around to play with.

But when Dana hit adolescence, things changed. Dana changed. One night Dana's mother called and talked to my stepdad for an hour. Finally he got off the phone.

"Dana's having some problems," he said quietly. "And her mom wants to get her away from the crowd she's running with." My stepdad paused. "Can we pull together for Dana and have her come live with us for a while?"

Mom was eager. "Sure we can."

"Of course," said Heidi.

I got this knot in my stomach. The decision clearly affected my life most. She'd have to transfer to my school, my grade. I played on the girls' basketball team; my friends were not a wild bunch. Some were athletes, all of them studied hard, a lot of them went to church. We respected our parents and followed the rules. That wasn't Dana's way. Why should her problems now be dumped on us?

"Where's she going to sleep?" I asked, hoping to nix the idea. The three bedrooms in our home were already occupied. "She can't live on the couch, can she?" Mom and my stepdad looked disappointed.

"My bedroom's the biggest," said Heidi. "She can share it with me." And so it was settled.

Winter 1994 was the most unpleasant season in the history of our home. Dana brushed in angrily that first night and hardly spoke, while Mom and Heidi fell all over themselves, helping her unpack and making her feel welcome. I hung back, watching, wondering when the big storm would come. I didn't have to wait long.

My stepdad poked his head in the bedroom door. "Let's all go for ice cream!"

"Count me out," Dana said. And she made it clear that she wasn't interested in any of our goody-two-shoes activities. My stepdad made her come anyway, and we all climbed into the car, none of us with an appetite for ice cream.

Later, alone in my bedroom, I went down on my knees. "Dear Lord, help us get through this. Change Dana so we can go back to normal." But my resentment grew when I heard Mom's footsteps hurrying down toward Heidi and Dana's room to wish them a good night.

Several mornings later I noticed dark circles around Mom's eyes. Because of all the chaos, she wasn't getting enough rest. "This is totally unfair," I complained to her.

"Things will get better," Mom said patiently. "Dana needs us." Mom took every opportunity to give her a compliment or a hug. And I wondered, how can Mom try so hard when Dana isn't trying at all?

Dinner at our house became a tense scene. Everyone seemed to be on edge. Gone were the animated conversations. Heidi was her chatty self, but I was definitely quieter. Mom and my stepdad had enough to worry about without listening to my frivolous teenage concerns, like the new outfit I coveted or how hard practice had been.

One night after doing the dishes, my stepdad and I went outside to shoot some baskets. While I had him alone, I thought I'd fill him in on what had been going on in my life since Dana's arrival. These days his focus always seemed to be on her. "I walk her to every class, introduced her to my friends, invited her to basketball games and to hang out. I've helped her with homework and explained school projects. What else am I supposed to do? What more does she want?"

My stepdad sighed. "I don't know, Haven," he said. "I just don't know." He bounced the ball. I wished I'd kept my mouth shut. Maybe my life wasn't affected most, after all.

For the first time I considered how Dana might be feeling. She'd moved into a new home, and switched midyear to a new school. It couldn't have been easy. I'd gone through the motions with her, but personally I'd pretty much kept my distance. Maybe that wasn't right. "God," I asked at bedtime, "help me to be more sisterly toward Dana."

My nightly prayers slowly but surely became more sincere. But the days always seemed to bring more nightmares. Why wouldn't God simply work a miracle and change Dana instantly? She'd been living with us for four long months, and I saw no end to the "temporary" setup.

Then something strange happened. On a night early in April, I was awakened from a sound sleep. I never wake up in the middle of the night. Never. Normally, a radio playing full blast couldn't wake me, but that night, at 1:00 A.M., something did. At the foot of my bed was an angel. He was clothed in pure white, with a bright light shining all around him. I couldn't see his face—it was surrounded by a sparkle—but when he spoke, his voice was deep, and urgent: "Tell her before it's too late."

"Tell who what?" I asked.

Reaching out toward me, he said again, "Tell her before it's too late."

I wasn't afraid, just completely puzzled. "Who?" I asked, mentally going down the list of my best friends' names. Who needed to hear something from me?

The deep-voiced angel simply repeated, "Tell her before it's too late." Then he was gone and my thoughts that night were full of questions. Why me?

I kept the angel's visit to myself. Who would believe me anyway? I wasn't even sure exactly what had happened—until two nights later.

He came back, this time even before I had fallen asleep. He appeared right beside my headboard and tapped my shoulder to get my attention. His message was the same, but even more urgent. "Tell her."

"Who?"

"Dana."

And he was gone.

In algebra the next day, I stared at the x's in the equations on the blackboard. What could I tell Dana? That I had been praying for God to change her radically and he was taking his time about it? Looking back, I had to admit she had made small efforts. She cheered at my basketball games, but I figured family was supposed to do that. She had pulled up her grades, though it was either that or be grounded. She was making friends of her own, including some pretty good kids, like Krystal, one of the cheerleaders. And at least she'd stopped bellyaching about going to church. Dana had even joined the choir, which Mom directed. Very un-Dana-like . . .

Now that I thought about it, things were much more pleasant at home. Dana had begun to change. I was the one who hadn't. I was as impatient as ever with God, and I suppose I was somewhat unwilling to share my parents' attention.

Maybe I needed to change some things about myself too.

That afternoon after school I did what I always did when I had a problem: I went to Mom. I told her about the angel's visits. "I know God loves me," I said.

"And I love Dana. But I still don't know what to tell her."

"Tell her how you feel," Mom said simply. "Tell her about God's love. Here's your chance to help your sister."

That evening, I got my courage up. "Dana," I said, "there's something I've got to tell you. Will you come on back to my room?" Dana looked at me skeptically. In all the time she'd lived with us, I don't think I'd ever invited her into my private sanctuary.

We sat on my bed. I was tense, not knowing how or where to begin. So I looked her straight in the eye and told her everything, about seeing an angel, about being sisters, and about God's love and how powerful it is. How we can do anything when we know it is for real. "The angel came because God cares about us," I told her. "He loves us." I began to cry and Dana reached out and hugged me. "I really care about what happens to you," I told her.

"I care about you too," she said.

I'd prayed for the change in Dana. But more importantly, God had changed me. I had asked him to touch one heart, and he took the opportunity to touch two.

A
Sister's
Strength

A ministering angel shall my sister be.
—WILLIAM SHAKESPEARE

SARAH

J. J. MCKENNA

I pause a little before picking up the cookie sheet. My half dozen cups of golden custard need only a touch of fire before becoming crème brûlée. But how much time under the broiler for a perfect disk to caramelize on the cream? "Oh, no," I groan. The recipe lets me down and doesn't say exactly how long under the fire. Sarah would know.

I think back three decades to when we were teens making fudge at our mother's stove. Three years older, Sarah stretched more than a head taller. Her height was just the first sign of other beauties to come. She grew into a gorgeous woman, a tall, thin blond with a Pepsodent smile. She's had the good fortune to keep her beauty too. Unlike most women with knock-out good looks, Sarah accepts her good fortune matter-of-factly. As a result, men feel free to admire her, and made-up women don't sense the comparison and so don't envy her. She's a natural.

"Not just yet," Sarah had cautioned. "You have to have the courage to leave it on the heat until just the right moment. If we don't cook it enough, we'll be eating our fudge with a spoon. But if we leave it on too long, the sugar will crystallize and maybe burn."

"But how will I know, Sarah?" I asked, even then an uncertain cook.

"Don't worry, Jen, you'll know. There, just now, see it thicken?" I did and I didn't. We poured it on a buttered platter and set it beside the grinning jack-o-lantern on the porch rail to harden in the cold October air. Sarah was right. Perfect fudge.

I pick up my sheet of custard cups and slide them into the oven remembering to check the time. Partly to time the cups and partly because I'm listening for the garage door to grumble as it opens and announce everyone's return from the hospital. Today's the day Sarah is released after surgery for breast cancer.

When I first heard the news, I cried through supper and into the evening. I almost wished it were me instead of Sarah, even though I knew I had to be here for my own daughter, Laura, now just a teen. That day, nothing Laura said would comfort me. But, then, how could I ask? Laura rode a roller coaster of her own. One day in love with the world and the next in despair over a boy's thoughtless betrayal. It seemed I had no recipe to help anyone I loved.

That night, sleep stayed just out of reach. I lay alone in bed and listened to the autumn winds buzz in the eaves. Cold weather was coming in. Then, for the first time in years, I heard a flock of Canadian geese calling—one to another—as they flew south on the crest of this early winter wind. I got up and watched them cross the silver circle of the moon. They traveled together, their calls reassuring each other, guided by instinct alone.

No sounds from the garage door just yet. I check the custards again. On them a ring of light brown begins to appear like a summer tan just beginning to glow. This sudden summer image makes me think of the day two summers ago when Sarah and I sat at the table in Mom's old kitchen. It's Sarah's kitchen now, because Sarah and Rob stayed on the farm and looked after Mom and Dad while I moved on to the city. Sarah and her husband have twin daughters, older than Laura and just into college. They seem to have grown effortlessly into fine young women, tall and blond and trusting like their mom.

That morning, Sarah held a mug of tea in her strong, supple hands, warming them to take off the early morning chill in the still cool kitchen. She looked inquiringly toward me, feeling instinctively my agony over how to raise my daughter, a girl with a tender heart.

"Wasn't it easier when we were growing up on the farm? No drugs, no booze, no cable TV, or internet freaks. Hardly any boys," I lamented, as I looked just past her shoulder at a picture of her and her girls splashing in the creek.

"Jen," Sarah fixed me with her eyes—our mother's eyes—emerald green freckled with brown, "raising a daughter, especially by yourself, isn't easy. With a child you never know when to step in or when to stand aside. And Laura won't tell you. I guess our twins did have an advantage. Not because they grew up in the country, though. It's because they had each other. You'll find the right way with Laura, though. You'll know it. You'll feel it."

But how? What I really need is a *Better Homes and Gardens* cookbook for raising kids, I wanted to scream. As I sat there, I felt the strength of her intuitive faith.

Later, back in the city, I took her words and tried to arrange them into verse. Most of the time, after teaching all day, I don't have the energy to write anything serious, although I've tried to keep a journal all these years. Sometimes on weekends, though, I find a little space in my head, where I lay out the pieces of my life like patches for a quilt. Sometimes these pieces of silk and denim and tulle come together to make a poem. If they do, I have always sent it, my home-stitched magic, to Sarah, my ideal reader.

So that September I wrote a poem and called it "Wind and Water." I am the tentative, invisible wind in the title, she the assured, mothering water. "You alternately stir and wait / believing that great food, like a great love, / comes half from knowing when to intercede / and half from letting things proceed on their own." These last lines were Sarah's as much as mine. She'd given me the pieces, unaware of the value of her gift. That Christmas, she hugged me and we danced an excited jig when the poem appeared in a literary journal.

Yikes! The crème brûlée! Heat rushes from the opened oven door. If I've ruined them . . . But no, the browned skin on top has only darkened into a lifeguard's late summer tan. They're still just fine.

Today I'm wearing my good sweats with a pumpkin appliqué that Sarah bought for me at a fall craft show. I've pinned a pink ribbon on it to honor her. Now I try to think of what to say when she comes in the door. Will I get it just right? Will I hold her too long and tight? Or will I try to seem too cheerful and bright?

Just now the garage door growls. They've arrived with Sarah. I check the crème brûlée. Perfect! Yes, fire changes things. Yet sometimes those things, those feelings, that pass through fire are the more beautiful for it. There's no recipe. No guarantee. You have to be ready. You have to trust that if perfect love has happened once, it can surely happen again. Sarah has always known that.

For there is no friend like a sister in calm or stormy weather
. . . to strengthen whilst one stands.
—CHRISTINA ROSSETTI

THE UNBREAKABLE BOND

SHARLENE SHARPE AND DARLENE GOODSON

A sat in the doctor's waiting room, thumbing nervously through a magazine, trying to focus on something besides the peculiar numbness in my legs. As I came upon an advertisement picturing identical twins, I lowered the page and smiled.

I was a twin myself—Sharlene, of Sharlene and Darlene, the Stegall twins. Darlene was not only my twin, she was my friend. We'd shared everything. Clothes, secrets, homework, boyfriends, tears. If Mom spanked one of us, both of us cried. When I got the mumps, Darlene got the mumps. That's why it seemed so strange when, at twelve, I got diabetes and she didn't.

The disease was discovered during a routine physical for summer camp. Darlene went to camp; I ended up in the hospital learning how to give myself insulin injections. As bad as that was, the worst pain was being separated from Darlene. Even today, both of us grown and with children, Darlene and I are still the best of friends, living in the same North Carolina town.

"The doctor will see you now," a nurse said. I followed her, strangely unsteady on my feet. This baffling numbness, which had started so abruptly, made me awkward and clumsy.

The doctor pricked my leg lightly with a needle. "Do you feel that?" he asked.

I shook my head.

"How about that?" he asked.

"No, nothing," I replied.

He frowned and scribbled something on my chart. As the examination ended, I tried to read the somber expression on his face.

"Sharlene," he said, "I'm going to be straight with you. Your diabetes is out of control. It's causing this muscle weakness in your legs. But that's only the tip of the iceberg. You've got neuropathy in your legs and feet, aneurysms in your eyes, and deteriorating kidneys. I'm afraid your body is wearing out."

Wearing out? This couldn't be true. I was only thirty-five. I knew the devastating toll diabetes could take, but I'd refused to believe anything would happen to me, at least not for a long time. "What can we do?" I cried. "I mean, surely you can do something to stop this!"

He lowered his eyes. "The truth is, there is almost nothing we can do. At this stage, diabetes always wins."

It was a diabetic's worst nightmare—wheelchair, blindness, dialysis, and eventually death. I sat there grimly, blinking into the doctor's face. I wanted to scream that it wasn't fair. It wasn't fair to me or to my husband, Gary, or to our two children. It wasn't fair!

The doctor went on talking about more tests, about seeing an eye specialist, but I scarcely heard him.

Driving home alone, I called on God. "Lord, please, isn't there some way I can get well? The doctor said I can't overcome diabetes. Dear Lord, if there's any way, it will have to be from you." I believed in God. I taught Sunday school. But I'd never asked for a miracle before. Where would I get that kind of faith?

At home I picked up the phone and dialed Darlene's number at work.

Darlene

As I listened to Sharlene over the phone, my heart sank. I'd been worried about her for days, but somehow I hadn't expected this. When we finally hung up I glanced at the pile of work on my desk. As a statistical assistant at the University of North Carolina, I had plenty to keep me busy, but there was no way I could concentrate. Instead I squeezed my eyes shut and did something unusual for me: I prayed. I really prayed. "God, please help my sister, I can't bear to see her slowly waste away. Please, won't you do something to save her?"

Sharlene and I had grown up going to church; but I had some tough setbacks over the years, and, frankly, my faith had taken some blows. There was my divorce, learning to be a single parent, the bouts of depression, the hospitalization. Through those difficult times, I couldn't perceive God's help and presence. Would it be different now?

I felt ashamed of my doubts; I wanted to believe. I really did. Sharlene, too, seemed to be having a hard time believing God could help her with something as big as this. Yet didn't Jesus say something about needing faith the size of a mustard seed to move a mountain? Maybe together Sharlene and I could come up with a mustard seed of faith. Maybe if we pooled our faith, shared it as we had shared everything else . . .

Sharlene

Gary and I drove to South Carolina to see my brother-in-law, an ophthalmologist in Charleston. During the long drive, I kept fighting an oppressive sense of despair. I thought of the prayer I'd prayed that day in the car, trying to believe God would answer it. Darlene said she had prayed too. Somehow just thinking that Darlene was praying made me feel better. It was as though her faith were nurturing mine.

I left Gary browsing through a big stack of magazines while I was examined. When it was over, he was waiting for me with a look of quiet excitement on his face and a rolled-up *Discover* magazine under his arm.

"Here," he said, holding it out to me. "Read this." He opened it, and there in big bold print were the words "Unshackled from Diabetes."

My eyes widened. The article told of the work of Dr. David Sutherland at the University of Minnesota Hospital; he was one of the few surgeons in the country performing pancreas transplants from live donors. I'd never heard of such a thing. In some cases, people were actually being cured of diabetes. There were risks. In fact, the pancreas was possibly the most difficult organ that surgeons had attempted to transplant.

My heart began to pound with a strange sensation. I read that there was a fifty percent rejection rate when a cadaver donor was used. But if the pancreas of a living, closely related donor was used, the rejection rate was only twenty-five percent. A living, closely related donor . . .

Gary voiced my thoughts: "You have an identical twin sister! Do you think Darlene would give you half her pancreas? Would she do that for you?"

At home I dropped my suitcase on the floor and ran to the phone. "Darlene, I'm about to ask you the most important question of our lives," I said. "Would you be willing to donate half your pancreas to me?"

Darlene didn't stop to think. "Sure," she said. Then, after a pause, she asked, "Can I live without it?"

I smiled on the other end. That was just like Darlene.

Darlene

I rolled a piece of paper into the typewriter and composed a letter to Dr. Sutherland. I told him how sick Sharlene was and said we were identical twins. I told him I wanted to give her half my pancreas.

You see, the strongest feeling came over me the day Sharlene asked me that "most important question." The words had barely got out of her mouth when I knew that God had sent us the answer we'd prayed for. He was sending a way to save her. This had to be it!

I mailed the letter that afternoon. We waited and wondered. Weeks went by. Finally I picked up the phone and called; Dr. Sutherland listened to me for nearly an hour. Then he said, "We'll have to run some tests to see if you're good transplant candidates. When can you both come to Minnesota?"

Our mustard seed of faith was beginning to sprout. But we still had a mountain to move.

Sharlene

When a package of information concerning the transplant arrived, I began to understand the risks involved in the surgery, not just for me, but for Darlene as well. We read it over together. There was the chance the surgery wouldn't work at all. And there were the usual risks in any surgery: death, brain damage from complications of being under anesthesia for six hours or more, hemorrhaging. We grew quiet as we scanned the long list.

"I don't know, Darlene," I said. "Maybe we should forget this."

"What do you mean? This is God's answer. How about having a little faith?" she countered.

I was still being surprised by the strength of my sister's faith.

"Forgetting for a moment the enormous risk in this, just how are we supposed to pay a hundred thousand dollars for these operations?" I asked Darlene. Her insurance company had already refused to participate on the grounds that my surgery was experimental and hers was elective.

My insurance company had not yet informed me of its decision. We knew that Dr. Sutherland's living-donor pancreas-transplant program was still new.

"God will take care of the little things," Darlene said.

Little? What had gotten into Darlene?

"Let's just go on faith," she added.

The magnetism of Darlene's faith, the brightness on her face, thawed something in me. "All right," I said. "We'll go on faith."

And that's what we did. In December we climbed on a plane for Minnesota, bound for two weeks of testing. The news was good. We were given a go-ahead for a transplant in the spring—May 13, 1987.

Darlene

With the date set, Sharlene was believing right with me that the transplant was God's answer to our prayers. And when her insurance company approved the surgery and decided to pay most of the costs, the answer seemed confirmed.

As the weeks of waiting dragged by, Sharlene's health deteriorated at a frightening pace. Her blood sugar raged out of control; the numbness in her legs was so advanced she could barely walk; she had one kidney infection after another; and her eyesight dwindled.

Meanwhile, circumstances in my own life took a turn for the worse. My eleven-year-old daughter, Chandra, became desperately ill with a rare kidney disease. I took her to Duke University for treatment. Every day, I walked from my motel room to the hospital, trying to hang on to the belief that God really would be there helping when the chips were down. But Chandra grew worse. My mustard seed of faith began to shrivel.

Just when my faith was nearly depleted, Sharlene arrived. We walked through a powdery snow to the hospital, Sharlene struggling to stay on her feet. Then, swoosh!

Her legs crumpled and she fell. "You should be home taking care of yourself," I told her, "not here with me."

"You don't think I'm going to let you go through this by yourself, do you? You chose to go through my pain with me; that's what I intend to do with you," she said, covered from head to foot with snow. "Besides, if I'm not here, who's going to help you keep the faith?"

After that, I felt my trust returning, a tangible, sometimes elusive assurance that God would take care of us, that I could leave the impossible to Him. It was amazing how catching faith could be.

As the days passed, Chandra improved; and when May arrived, Sharlene and I checked into the hospital in Minnesota for the transplant, our faith in full bloom. But it didn't take long for me to discover how fear can nip even the strongest blossoms.

The night before surgery, Sharlene hobbled down the hospital corridor to my room in the donor wing and found me sitting in the middle of the bed, hugging my knees and crying. I hated for her to see me like that, but while going through the extensive preparations for surgery, face-to-face with all the risks, the enormity of what I was about to undergo crashed in. "Oh, Sharlene, I'm so scared," I cried. "I don't know if I can do it."

She put her arms around me. "We don't have to go through with it," she told me. "We can go home. It's all right."

I looked at my sister through a wash of tears. I remembered her sliding around on her hands and knees in the snow, and I was filled with love. So much love. It made me determined to hang on. "No, I want to do it," I said. "In spite of this awful fear, I want to do it. I still believe this is God's answer."

Sharlene's husband, Gary, and our pastor joined us, and the four of us held hands and prayed. We asked God to renew our faith and give us the strength to go through with the surgery. We asked him to be with us every step of the way.

The next morning they wheeled us into the operating room together. The last thing I remember was holding Sharlene's hand.

Sharlene

As I awoke, I stared at an IV bottle hanging over my head. I lay still, wondering if I would feel different with part of Darlene's pancreas inside my body. Slowly I became aware of the most remarkable sensation. I could feel the sheets on the back of my legs. I could feel my legs! I knew, long before the doctors knew, that the diabetes was gone.

Darlene

I peered at the clock on my hospital wall. It was two-thirty A.M., nearly ten days since the surgery. For no reason, I'd awakened from a sound sleep. My recovery had been slow for days I'd wandered in and out of consciousness. But soon Sharlene and I would be going home. The doctor said the transplant was a complete success, that she should live practically a normal life now.

There in the dark spaces of the night, I took time to marvel at the power of just a little faith, at what a mighty thing it is—especially when it is shared. Neither Sharlene nor I had perfect faith. But both of us tried to offer what we had to the other, and somehow, in the sharing of it, trust in God was born and reborn.

Suddenly I heard a sound at my door, and looking up, I saw Sharlene. "I woke up and figured you might be awake too," she said.

I slid over, and she slipped into the bed, just as if we were little girls again.

"I love you, Darlene," Sharlene said suddenly.

"And I love you," I told her.

She looked at me a long moment. "I know," she whispered, "I know."

An Olympic skater's sister has strength for everyone.

JANE

DAN JANSEN

he worst thing about Jane dying when she did is that too many people will remember her only as a tragedy of the 1988 Olympics, or as the sister of Dan Jansen. I want her to be remembered as a person in her own right, someone with hopes and dreams, with faults and frailties, with special qualities.

Jane Jansen was the seventh of Harry and Geraldine Jansen's nine children. She was three-and-a-half years older than Mike and five years older than me, the baby of the family. In such a large unit there are inevitably going to be "the older kids" and "the younger kids," and Jane, Mike, and I definitely made up the latter group. We were the tagalongs, the ones without all the responsibility. (Joanne, who was born two years before Jane, always complains that she was a "swing kid," too young to be an older kid, too old to be a younger kid.) Jane was easily the most sensitive Jansen, the one most attuned to other people's feelings and most vulnerable to criticism from the outside. I'm like Jane in a lot of respects (although I never cried as much, on the outside, as she did) in that I'm sensitive to the way people feel about me, though I try not to show it.

Naturally, Mike and I, being boys, were not above exploiting Jane's sensitivity. We'd make her cry, which was never hard to do, but she always forgave us. One of the legendary Jansen-kid stories, which my mother never tires of telling, was when Jane fell asleep on the couch and Mike and I put chocolate chips all over her to see if they would melt. They did. When Jane woke up, she cried. When Mom got home she hollered, mostly, I think, because in a house with so many kids it was a crime to waste chocolate chips.

Jane was never cruel to anyone. Never. It was not in her nature. She was one of those people who was so nice, in fact, that you wondered if she was for real. Later, when Jane was dying, Diane, the fourth oldest, apologized to her for all the times she had hollered at her when they were kids. "Oh, Di, that didn't make any difference," Jane told her. "You were just being a mother to us." Four of my five sisters are nurses, but only Jane was too homesick to live at nursing school, which was only a few miles from home. And no matter how much we teased her, Jane was always ready to drive Mike and me wherever we wanted to go.

Jane was tough in her own way, though. When she was fourteen she developed scoliosis and had to wear a brace. She followed the doctor's orders religiously and only took that thing off for showers. She often slept on the couch because the brace was so uncomfortable and all she did was toss and turn. But she never complained. . . .

Jane met her husband, Rich Beres, at a softball party. They had three children. My oldest brother, Jim, always says that Jane wanted only two things out of life—to be a nurse and a mother—so in that respect, she died satisfied. There's a lot of truth to that. But it would be ridiculous to call what happened to her anything but a tragedy.

On January 29, 1987, Jane gave birth to her third daughter, Jessica. Mary delivered Jessica, as she did several other of her nieces. Everything seemed normal. My parents got the word in Quebec, where they were watching me compete in a world sprint meet. When they returned they went directly from the airport to congratulate Jane and kiss their new granddaughter. There was some vaguely disturbing news, however. A routine blood test had discovered something, and Jane was asked to come back to the hospital. By that time I was home for a week before returning to

Europe for the remainder of the World Cup season. On the morning of February 4, Jane got the news: she had leukemia.

I remember coming home that morning after working out, and, for reasons I can't remember, Bonnie Blair was with me. Probably she was just stopping over to say hello to the family, whom she had known for some time. I knew that Jane had gone in for tests, but I hadn't really paid it much mind since she was such a healthy, athletic person. She had played a game of volleyball the night before she gave birth, after all. Dad and my oldest brother, Jim, were in the living room, and right away I knew something was wrong when I saw Dad with red eyes.

"They've diagnosed Jane with leukemia," said Jim, the member of the family least likely to mince words.

. . . Maybe it'll go away, I thought as I drove to Jane's. Maybe it's all a bad dream. Maybe the tests are wrong. But when I entered the house and saw all my brothers and sisters and in-laws, and then I saw Jane, I knew it was true. We held each other for a long time. Later I found out what Jane's first reaction had been. "Oh, my God, Rich," she said to her husband. "I'm going to die and you'll have to take care of the kids alone." Besides Jessica, her other daughters, Susie and Amy, were only three and one-and-a-half years old.

Nobody was ready to give up, of course. My mother had already dug out the textbooks and was doing her research. And I honestly believe that right up until the end, which was a little more than a year from that awful day, Jane believed she could beat it. Then, too, we were all deeply religious people, not the kind who preached about miracles on street corners, but people with a deep and abiding belief in God. However, a sense of reality pervaded the family. My mother and four of my sisters, including Jane, were nurses; Mary was working at the hospital where Jane had been tested and had seen the worried looks that passed between the doctors when they got the results. My father was a policeman, and so were two of his sons and one of his daughters. And Jane's husband, Rich, was a fireman. People in those kinds of jobs deal with reality every single day of their lives. Nobody spoke openly about it, not in the beginning anyway, but we all knew that Jane's fight was going to be long, hard, and, in the end, probably futile.

One of the first things to be done with a leukemia patient is to find a match for a bone marrow transplant. As luck would have it, both Joanne and I were perfect. I was in Europe for a World Cup meet by the time the match was discovered and immediately wrote Jane a letter telling her that I'd be more than willing to be the donor. Later, that got a lot of attention, as if I deserved credit for it. That's absurd. . . . The decision to use Joanne made a lot of sense, even though I meant every word of what I told Jane in [the] letter.

In that letter I also remember apologizing for all the problems I had unloaded on her over the years. Being away from family so much of the time in Europe and facing the constant pressure of competition can be hard on the mind, and Jane was the one I leaned on. My problems were never insurmountable ones, and the death of a loved one makes you realize that fact even more. But you're not thinking about anything but yourself when you're feeling down and alone and eating strange food in a boardinghouse where no one speaks English. In retrospect, I suppose that was the most unusual thing about the bond between Jane and me. I could always talk to her, and I think that's rare for brother and sister. But that's just the way Jane was.

❧❧❧

Believe it or not, I was healthy through much of the 1987–1988 season. I was healthy, and my sister was dying of leukemia. . . . One point I must emphasize is that, had Jane been near death when it was time for me to leave, there is no way I would've gone. But a few days after I left, her condition gradually worsened and kept getting worse. This made it extremely hard on my family. They held a big meeting to decide who would go to Calgary and who would stay home. Jane, of course, told everybody to go, including my mother. Mom was torn. She desperately wanted to stay home, but Jane kept insisting she go to Calgary. Finally, Diane met privately with Jane and said to her, "Look, you know you want Mom here. So tell her. Otherwise, she might go to Calgary because she thinks you want her to." So at last Jane told my mom to stay, and both of them were very relieved.

Eventually, Mary, Janet, Jim, and various husbands and children drove to Calgary in three vans, and my dad flew up. On February 13, the day before the 500, Jane's lungs started to fill with fluid and the situation turned grave. I remember my father coming up to me after I finished training that day and saying, "I'm needed at home. Try to hang in there." The others wanted to go home, too, but Mom decided that I needed some support up there and they stayed.

Dad arrived at O'Hare Airport in Chicago at about eleven-thirty P.M. and still had to drive home from there. During his flight Jane's condition had worsened and there was some thought that she was going to die before he made it. But Mom said, "No, she'll wait for her father." He got to the hospital at about two A.M. and spent some time with her. Up in Calgary, I knew that things were bad but couldn't be sure how bad. But by this time the rest of the family knew she was going to die that day. I wrote in my journal that night:

This is it, D.J. Do it for Jane. You, and everyone else in the family.

At about five-thirty A.M. the family was called back to the hospital. The end was near, and all wanted to say their final goodbyes. It was February 14, the morning of the five-hundred-meter race. At six-thirty A.M. everyone went in, individually, and had a moment. Jane's husband made sure that Mary, Janet, and Jim were called in Calgary, and there was only a brief discussion about whether or not to tell me.

"Everyone else had their time with Jane," said Diane, and Dan should too." I don't think they would've ever forgiven themselves if I hadn't had my moment. I had said goodbye to Jane when I had left for Calgary one week earlier, but she had still been doing pretty well then. So it was by no means a proper goodbye.

They called me at about six A.M., Calgary time. There was a knock on the door, and Brian Wanek, one of my teammates, told me I had a phone call. I knew it had to be something bad—six-A.M. phone calls are rarely anything good—and I woke up Nick, who was rooming with me and said, "It must be Jane."

I remember running down the hall to take the elevator to the basement—that's where the phone was—and I was shaking all over. I couldn't stop. It gets a little fuzzy at this point, but I think I talked to Mike first and then to my mother, who explained that Jane's blood pressure was dropping fast and that she probably wouldn't make it through the day.

"We want you to say goodbye, Dan," my mother told me. "Jane won't be able to respond, but she will be able to understand you."

I don't remember exactly what I said, but I told her I loved her and that I was going to win the race that night for her, even though I didn't believe it myself. There was not much else to say. My sister was dying and I was helpless, so far away from her. I couldn't hear a sound, not even the whir of the respirator she was hooked up to. Later, Diane and Joanne told me that they were positive Jane heard me because she breathed on her own while I was talking. I hope so. I really hope so.

. . . The funny thing is, I am absolutely positive I did the right thing. I have no regrets about skating, and I would certainly make the same decision again. But I would try to be more positive about it, to turn the warm feelings I had toward Jane into something forceful and to let myself know that it was okay to compete at the same time I was grieving. But that's easy to say now. I don't think anyone confronted with this situation could deal with it rationally the first time.

The rest of the day is a blur. We had a team meeting in one of the rooms, and the guys decided to dedicate their races to Jane. That meant a lot to me, so of course I started crying again and so did a few of my teammates. After that, Nick and I went for a little jog around the Village and I remember being really startled about how quickly the news had spread. A few people even came up to me and said, "Why did they tell you? Why didn't they just let you skate?" That made no sense. I was bound to hear the news, as they had, and I certainly wanted to get it from my loved ones. And I wanted to have that last conversation with Jane.

The race was set for early evening, 5:10 P.M., prime time back in the United States, so it could be televised. I didn't do anything different in my pre-race preparation, but I distinctly remember that when I got onto the ice, I felt like I hadn't been on skates in six months. The best way I can describe it is wobbly, like someone who wasn't used to skating. Thoughts raced through my head and stuck there, like giant roadblocks. Jane is dead. Should I be here? Jane is dead. What does everyone think about me skating? Jane is dead. How hard must this be for my parents, watching me on TV and facing the prospect of what must be the absolutely worst thing in life—burying a child? Jane is dead.

Under other circumstances, I would've felt confident. I was in excellent physical condition and was coming off a series of terrific performances. Going into the race, and without considering the emotional weight I was carrying around, the two favorites were Uwe-Jens Mey, my good friend from East Germany, and me. There were a few good Japanese skaters, too, and the usual formidable Russians. But at any rate I was definitely being counted on for a medal.

I drew the first inner turn for my race, meaning that I finished on the outside. That was the desirable draw because, as I said before, it's easier to have the final outer when you're at your highest rate of speed. If you look at clips from some five-hundred-meter races on fast ice, in fact, you'll see guys coming out of that last inner turn going way out into the outer lane. It's almost funny to watch, unless you happen to be the skater.

The only thing I remember about being at the starting line is that I wasn't focused on the race—a fatal flaw, to say the least. To a person, my whole family, those at the Games and those watching at home, said I looked like a ghost, all the color drained from my face. My mother was absolutely convinced that she was correct to have told me to skate until she saw me at the line. "My God," she said. "What have we asked him to do?" Everything seemed to be happening as if in a dream, and I just couldn't get myself to concentrate.

When I looked at the videotape later, the ABC commentator was saying, "The eyes of the world are focused on Dan Jansen," but I had no perception of what was happening to me. The best way to describe the final part of that awful tragic day is through my journal. Oddly, I have no memory of writing the entry for February 14, 1988. I must've gone back to my room after the five hundred and used it as a kind of therapy. The words still bring tears to my eyes today:

When I got to the line, I don't remember what I was thinking but I know that when the starter said "ready," I wasn't. I wasn't the same as usual, ready to blast off the line and kick everyone's butt.

Then I jumped [false-started], which is rare for me.

I waited on the second start and got off slow. The 100 was terrible, I was slipping, I couldn't power it like I usually do. 9.9 for me is hideous—I should've been 9.6 or 9.7.

I set the turn up OK, but in my second stroke, my left outer might as well have been on a banana peel. It just didn't hold me at all.

What a day! Good night, Jane. Rest in peace.

Stronger than a man, simpler than a child,
her nature stood alone.

−CHARLOTTE BRONTË

A HOLE IN THE HEAD

BRENDA PETERSON

"Promise me," my sister said, taking my hand, "that if the surgery fails, you won't let me linger on without a mind. Promise me you'll let me go."

My middle sister, Paula, knew well the risks of this delicate neurosurgery—she had even diagnosed herself. The youngest surgical instructor in the operating room at Emory University in Atlanta, Paula was twenty-two in 1974. With the black humor typical of her OR colleagues, Paula joked that the only reason she'd allow herself to go "under the knife" of her peers was because she needed a job.

"Last time I scrubbed in," she laughed, "I fainted during surgery. When I awoke, the patient and I were lying side by side in the recovery room. 'What happened to you?' the surgeon I was scrubbing in with asked. 'It wasn't my humming, was it?' 'No,' I told him, 'it was my head.' 'Well, you need to get that head of yours fixed before you operate again in this unit.'"

Since childhood, my sister's head had been a source of amazement and, for us sisters, income. Paula and I charged other kids a nickel apiece to touch the base of her skull, which was as soft and eerily yielding as a newborn's. Like an infant's soft spot, my sister's "hole in the head" inspired awe and some tenderness, even among grade schoolers more impressed with species of spiders and snakes than anything human. Touching Paula's soft skull was like entering a forbidden place, an opening in the skull that was supposed to close over any day now but never did; we children could put our hands on a secret that our bodies understood long before we might grasp it with our minds: Some wounds won't heal, no matter what adults say.

In 1957, when Paula was five, we first discovered the hole in her head. Doctors diagnosed it as a hematoma, or a swelling filled up with extravasated blood. A budding science student, I diligently looked up the definition of "extravasate," as my sister gazed over my shoulder.

"'. . . to force out from the proper vessels, as blood . . .'" Paula read *sotto voce* with the dramatic flair that would one day make her star of high school plays. "Or, 'to pour forth . . . like lava.'"

"Lava!" my three-year-old sister, Marla, giggled. "A volcano blowed up in her brains!"

From then on it was "brain lava" we advertised in our freak peep show and we upped the charge to a dime for kids to touch Paula's soft skull. Two decades later when Paula called me with the news of her impending neurosurgery, she asked, "Remember the brain lava theory of our childhood? Well, I don't think we were too far off, although none of the docs here agree with my diagnosis. I think it's a very rare *sinus para crania*, or an outpouching of the circulatory system of the brain through a hole in the skull."

"Hole in the head," I echoed softly and tried not to cry long distance. "Is it dangerous?" We had become so accustomed to my sister's soft spot. Perhaps her vulnerability was what drove Paula to be the daredevil among us—doing triple flips from high dives while we other sisters played it safer with gymnastics and uneven bars on the ground. In our minds, her hematoma was no more than a birthmark. One doesn't go about risking one's life to fix a birthmark no one could see anyway.

"Very dangerous," she said, "but you can't tell anybody. If it is a brain tumor, I could wake up a vegetable." She paused and laughed. "Do vegetables ever really wake up?"

"You'll wake up," I assured her, but my voice was shaking. I willed myself to be strong for my younger sister, to protect her from my fears for her. All our childhood Paula and I had been each other's bodyguards against the vagaries of a manic-depressive, often violent mother and a father whose long absences we explained to each other as "missing in action." Because our father didn't protect us, Paula and I took the role of pint-sized commanders-in-chief on the home front. Together we older sisters kept the weather watch on Mother's emotional storm. . . .

"I'm not telling Mom and Dad the truth," Paula said slowly, as if she'd just made her decision. "I'll only say it's routine surgery. You mustn't let them know how risky this is."

I didn't argue. The last thing my sister needed was to worry about soothing my parents, guarding them when she herself was in danger.

"They'll be no help anyway," Paula finished, her voice cracking. "But I want you there with me, especially since Dad said he's 'just a phone call away' and is only sending Mother. And you know Simon. He says he's got a cold and can't fly up here. I think he doesn't want to marry a woman with a hole in her head. So promise me you'll come."

I made my promises in the three days before that neurosurgery. The first was not to ask so many questions; the last was that I would take responsibility for "pulling the plug," as my sister called it. I also made many promises to my kindhearted boss, Harriet Waldon, of *The New Yorker* magazine, who granted me leave from my editorial assistant job without question. This mother hen to our department was one of the few people I told about the seriousness of my sister's surgery. Waving her cigarette and tapping my forehead with a strong forefinger, she said, "You just go. You don't ask 'Why, God?' You just sit in that waiting room and hold on to her with your heart. Look at me, all my friends are so old, their second homes are operating rooms—that's why I'll never give up smoking." She offered me a Doral cigarette and told me story after successful surgical story. I memorized these survivors' tales; later, during the twelve hours of waiting to hear if my sister would survive neurosurgery intact, I repeated Mrs. Walden's stories back to myself like living mantras.

Though I was well into writing my first novel, though I'd come from a long line of lively Southern storytellers, it wasn't until I sat in the pale green waiting room of an Atlanta hospital that I fully felt the power of stories to hold so fierce a lifeline for myself, for my sister. And this umbilical cord, this story line, was a strong connection not only while my sister slept under the scalpel, but also the night before her surgery.

I flew down that night from New York City to find Paula in her kitchen, consumed with the chore of repapering her cupboards. "I've packed for a short stay," she said, cutting huge swatches of bright contact paper. "Our father is just a phone call away, and our mother is done in with a migraine over at a church friend's house."

"Out for the count," I said. "Why are you fiddling with your kitchen? Shouldn't we be . . . well, doing something more meaningful?"

"You want to administer my last rites?" Paula laughed. In the fluorescent kitchen light her face was full of shadows I'd never seen before. I shivered inwardly, though the night was humid, clinging. Everything felt dingy, inside and out. This was not the way I'd imagined we should spend what might be our last night together. I'd wanted some important event, so we could both face the surgery girded with the heroic armor of a soldier the night before battle. But here we were papering her kitchen shelves—what kind of flimsy shield was this with which to fend off death?

"Simple tasks," my sister said, reading my mind as usual. "They teach us in nursing school—no heroics, just everyday chores to remind us that we'll be here tomorrow to finish what we start. I intend to leave these shelves half done, so I'll have to wake up. God knows, honey, you'd never paper shelves, even if it was a way of mourning me, even if I bequested them to you in my will—'And to my beloved sister I leave . . . my kitchen shelves!'"

We laughed and slathered the cupboard with Super Glue in the corners where the paper was already curling up. I realized this was the first time we had really laughed since news of the surgery. Soon we were even singing in our familiar two-part harmony as we worked long past midnight.

I picked up a roll of shelf paper as my partner and I began a delicate two-step dance. She joined in the dance from the shelves and we danced for some time before we remembered what awaited us the next morning.

That night we slept together as we had much of our childhood: she curled up with a pillow to her belly where she once held her dolls, my body fitted against her back, one arm lightly encircling her as if I could still spare her the bad dreams, the savage days, of our childhood. She whispered to me as she fell asleep what she would tell me the next morning as the nurses wheeled her to surgery: "I won't die young. We'll be papering kitchen shelves together when we're ninety." . . .

My sister Paula had indeed diagnosed herself. When the neurosurgeon and a doctor friend of my sister's returned after the eight-hour operation, they were subdued, their faces dark. My heart pounded so hard I could barely hear the neurosurgeon, who seemed to be very angry at his young associate. . . .

"Quite a mess." Dr. Carkeek shook his head.

"But did she . . . is she okay?" I grabbed the bedstand and felt faint. A post-op nurse had called my mother and me in the waiting room to say there was a problem;

we should return to Paula's hospital room and wait for her until further report. My anxious mother succumbed to a migraine, which kept her groggy, vague. . . .

When they at last wheeled Paula in, I was unprepared for the sight of her: lips swollen blue-black from the breathing tubes, bruises all over her arms from the IVs and elbows of operating room staff; but the worst was over her head. They'd shaved a wide patch of her long hair and bandaged the back of her skull; but my sister had already hidden her wound under a patch of her abundant blond hair.

"Bride of Frankenstein, Behba," my sister managed to say through thick lips, using her pet name for me. "Eight-inch incision, like somebody hit me over the head with a pickax. Not a pretty sight these wire stitches . . . but I'm awake, ain't I?"

She didn't stay awake for long. Dr. Carkeek was worried about post-op seizure, so he prescribed a heavy dose of Valium for the night. Whether it was the drugs, to which all of my family are extremely sensitive, or post-op psychosis common in these cases, my sister's first night after surgery was horrific. Incoherently she thrashed about in her bed until the night-shift nurses tied her down. Paula wept and ground her teeth like an animal clamped tight in a steel trap. I held her hand as I wondered—was the trap also the steel sutures tugging tightly in a crisscross gash down her skull? I tried to calm her by massaging her feet, the only part of her body not bruised. . . .

That night in the hospital as I sat with my sister Paula, watching her thrash about in her drugged sleep, I sang her the songs of our shared childhood. I had to imagine my sister's harmonies to support me. And in that deep dark with my moaning sister, I comforted myself with the memory of Paula telling me, "When I sing, Behba, I always hear you, too, even if you're not with me."

The next morning's angiogram extended Paula's trauma. . . . My sister, still not yet fully conscious after the previous night's Valium dose, screamed out in pain and fought the technicians who, without doctor's orders, followed normal procedure for someone presurgery, injecting her with an IV push—an intravenous dose of Valium made much stronger by the direct influx of drug into the bloodstream. Immediately my sister calmed, but the IV push sent her into a Valium overdose and a semi-coma. Because Paula had chosen to have this neurosurgery performed at a hospital in Tennessee, she was not safeguarded by the usual insider status accorded a staff nurse at her own Emory Hospital in Georgia. . . .

Since we couldn't get ahold of Paula's neurosurgeon, it was to my sister's doctor and nurse friends I now turned for advice and treatment, though they had no power to prescribe or take over her case. Paula was not only in a coma, she was also in medical limbo in which we all had to wait until we found her doctor to take any action to help her.

I was in a rage of confusion and fear. The first call was to my sister Marla, whose gift at explaining the medical word-salad to a layperson is unparalleled from her years working as an intensive care nurse.

"Talk to her, sis!" Marla ordered. "Hearing and touch are the last to go. So hold on to her and talk, sing, tell dirty doctor jokes—anything to anchor her attention. Don't let her just float. That's when they all take off. You know, comas are strange. Sometimes I think a coma is like mandatory attendance in some class you skipped out of in daily life. It's not just time out. I think coma patients are in an unconscious study hall." Marla paused, then said gently, "She's not going to die, Behba. I can feel her still kicking, all the way up here in Pittsburgh! Besides, what would we do without our middle sister? It's supposed to be this way: the Three Musketeers, the three-legged stool, third time's the charm. The numbers ain't right for Pooh to go. She's got to stay with us, it's natural.

As Marla said it, I felt the truth of it. We three sisters were another eternal triangle, as strong and profound a balancing act as the triangle of mother, father, and child. . . .

I took a deep breath and gazed at Paula's unconscious, upturned face. In the small halo thrown from the bed lamp, her pale hair pulled back to cover a white head bandage, she looked at last peaceful, even radiant. . . . For the first time since she'd come out of surgery, I began to weep. I knew that it was safe now to cry with my other sister on the phone, holding the lifeline that I hadn't been able to let go ever since they wheeled Paula into the operating room.

Marla's voice was so soothing as she said, "Put the phone in Pooh's ear, Behba, and let me talk to that girl. I've got a few things to say might wake her up!"

I held the phone to Paula's unconscious ear and shook with quiet sobs. At last, someone else to help me keep my sister in the world. My other sister. I watched Paula's eyelids flickering, the rapid eye movements of otherworldly dreams, as deep inside her coma she listened.

It was only then, when the tears had relaxed me enough to ease my terror and help me think straight, that I remembered Paula herself had had notable success in her own neurosurgical nursing work with coma victims; she always talked and read to them, touched them and told them it was time to come back. Once she established a code system of squeezing fingers with a small comatose boy who over a period of six months kept contact with her until he at last opened his eyes. "I watched you from up there," he had told Paula. "I was floating on the ceiling and I didn't want to come back down to my body. It hurt."

As Marla talked a blue streak into Paula's ear, I tried to remember that finger code to crack this coma. Right then I actually longed for our mother to be in this hospital room. She had been a telegrapher during the war for the Wabash railroad and her fast, brilliant fingers were the talk of the rails. Maybe her Morse code would rouse Paula? As I gently tapped Paula's open palm, I heard Marla's tiny voice calling my name.

"Listen," she said when I cradled the phone on my shoulder. "Tonight is crucial.

If we can catch her before she slips too deep, we've got her. Can you stay awake another night? Do you want me to fly down tomorrow morning?"

"Yes," I said, again giving way to tears. "I'm so sleepy . . ."

Then Marla went into action. She arranged for some of Paula's nurse friends to travel up to that Tennessee hospital and set up round-the-clock shifts with Paula. I don't remember much of that night except sitting with Sherrie Scott, Paula's best friend from college, and the radiator hissing. Sherrie talked a blue streak to Paula, telling her stories of their college days as bawdy and entertaining as *The Canterbury Tales*. There were others who relieved me, young doctors and nurses, Paula's hospital colleagues. . . .

By the next evening, Paula began to tremble like an animal in the twitches and horizontal kicks of a running dream. Within minutes, her luminous blue eyes shot open and she bounded halfway out of bed like a prisoner escaping. Sherrie and I caught her in our arms, laughing and screaming for joy. . . .

For another half a day Paula would lapse into coma and then leap out of it like the old gymnast that she was. Sometimes we simply sat on her legs to keep her in the bed. She murmured and moaned to herself and yelled at us for keeping her flat. Then, very slowly as we entered the second evening of coma alternating with incoherent consciousness, Paula suddenly sat up in bed and did not try to run away. . . .

I lived in the hospital with her all week while she recovered from both the neurosurgery and its aftermath. Marla decided another nurse was unnecessary and she would come be with Paula after she was released from the hospital. My mother visited daily before returning to play with her friends; and my father, as always, was just "a phone call away."

During one of her better days, I asked Paula, "Did you hear us talking to you in your coma?"

Then Paula grinned. "Yeah, it was a real talk show in there, Behba. I thought you'd never shut up. And Mo . . . if I weren't in a coma I'd be downright embarrassed by some of those traveling salesmen dirty jokes she told me. I was laughing my head off. . . ." She gingerly touched her bandage. "Oops, wrong metaphor."

"Did you feel my finger codes?" I asked.

Paula nodded and gave me a fond look. "You remembered, Behba. Do you know what your message was saying?"

"No, just gibberish, I suppose."

"You were saying, yes, yes, yes, yes, yes, yes, yes!" Paula laughed. "My finger code with that coma kid was simple: yes and no. 'Yes' was a quick squeeze and 'no' was a long squeeze. Next time I think I'll teach you sign language so at least you can be more eloquent." She grew more serious and held out her arms to embrace me. "Although," she murmured, holding me tight, "'yes' says it all, doesn't it, honey?"

Through the Eyes of a Baby Sister

To have a loving relationship with a sister is not simply to have a buddy or confidante—it is to have a soul mate for life.
–VICTORIA SECUNDA

TO MY SISTER

PATRICIA VOLK

Beaming down the high school corridor, my big sister comes toward me. Why is she laughing so hard? Nearing her, I can see: She is wearing my blouse! The blouse I saved for months to buy. The blouse I've never worn. She's stolen it out of my closet. If rage could kill, I would be dead.

Born eighteen months apart, my sister and I fought daily. Knives were thrown. My right thumb was slammed in a door. Circle fights were the worst. Trapped in a room, we'd hiss and snarl, picking weapons to maim each other with hangers, hairbrushes, shoes—whatever we could grab without breaking the circle. Eventually, my sister won. She always did.

"Someday you'll love her," my mother said with a smile.

"I wish she was dead," I'd snap.

And yet, and yet . . .

Punished together, banished to our room, we were instant allies. We plotted escape. We wrote musicals and did the cancan. We midwifed guppies so they wouldn't eat their young. We developed our own language: A penis was a linga-linga. Tonguey-lungies were two cubes of meat still attached to a ligament some grown-up had sloppily cut for us. When our parents spoke French so we wouldn't understand, we made up our own French:

Shock on voo shawn on tain.

Instun tain on poo sha.

"Why did you beat me up so much when we were little?" I ask my sister.

"What did you do that made me?" she replies.

I know some sisters who only see each other on Mother's Day and some who will never speak again. But most are like my sister and me, treasurers of each other's childhoods, linked by volatile love, best friends who make other best friends ever so slightly less best.

"Sisters have a more intense relationship than two brothers or a brother and a sister," says Pat Heller, a family therapist with the Ackerman Institute for Family Therapy in New York. "Women in general have much more of a tradition to be intimate and actually talk things out. There's also more intense competition. The stakes are higher the more intimate you are."

The nicest thing my sister said to me in the first seventeen years of my life was, "Hey, your legs really aren't so bad."

And yet, and yet . . .

I can't see myself without seeing her. Thanks to my sister, I consider myself short. I may be five-feet-seven, but she's five-feet-nine. Since she's a great athlete, I'm not. When it was her turn to serve in volleyball, the game was over. I played right field with the glove over my nose, terrified a fly ball would hit it.

Despite our differences, people called us the Volk Girls. To minimize sibling rivalry, our parents developed categories: My sister was the pianist, I was the singer. My sister was the scholar, I was the clown. She was the dancer, I was the artist. Ironically, this bred competition.

"Your sister leans into the curve better than you do," Dad shouts as I sit behind him on his motorcycle. Now every time a curve comes I think, Am I leaning as well as my sister? At family [get-togethers], an ancient scenario gets reenacted: My father asks my mother to dance. Then he asks my sister. Then he doesn't ask me. Then my mother whispers to him. Then he asks me.

My sister's grace, athleticism, and academic excellence forced me to forge my own path. I became a painter. I perfected my swan dive. I mastered a stringed instrument made out of goat bladder and had intense relationships with boys who hated their mothers.

When I was lucky enough to join her magic circle, she kept things exciting in ways I never dreamed of.

"I'm bored," she'd yawn, and people would vie to amuse her. On weekends she had three dates a night: the date, the late date, and the late, late date. She was the party doll. I searched for soul.

The months that separated us were the Grand Canyon. Or was it simply that we were sisters, doomed to polarities, modeling ourselves against each other? My sister is on the boards of seven organizations. So I wear Eau de Stay Away. My sister puts on jewelry to go jogging. I once left the house wearing two different shoes. As a therapist my sister gushes words, using them to soothe, heal, and reframe. As a writer, I scrape sentences for truth, treating words like grenades; life hangs on each one. My sister would never buy used furniture. I would never buy new.

And yet, and yet . . .

I show her my $3 tag sale chairs. I've screwed a walnut into the top of each one. "Look," I point to the nuts. "Nature's finial."

And it turns out that at the moment I was screwing walnuts into chairs in New York, my sister was setting fake rubies into chairs in Miami.

Two thousand miles apart, we both decide to get pedicures and we both pick Redford Red.

When I slice the end off my finger with a kitchen gadget, my sister says, "I did the exact same thing last year!"

Being an older sister, she bandaged it herself and never bothered to tell me. Being a younger sister, I called her from the emergency room at Roosevelt Hospital, where the top hand surgeon in New York was taking care of me. Thanks to birth order, my sister has something I'll never have: a need to be brave. And I have something she'll never have: a powerhouse to be inspired by.

"Do you realize we can do anything?" my sister says.

She's a licensed scuba diver. So now I am too. Last month she got me kayaking. Now I'm considering buying an Aquaterra kayak of my own. This morning she called:

"I want you to think about something."

"What?" I feel like I'm falling.

"I want you to take five days off and come down here and we'll kayak six hours a day."

Six hours a day? In a kayak? Can I do that? I'll have to ask my sister. Because she thinks I can do something, sometimes I can.

Which doesn't mean she can't still make me crazy:

In a restaurant, I wipe sleep out of my eye and she gasps, "That's repulsive!"

"What?"

"Don't you realize what you're doing?"

"Well, *excuuuuuse* me. I had something in my eye."

We are sharing a Cobb salad. A huge bowl is between us. My sister is picking out the blue cheese. The blue cheese is vanishing. I wasn't going to say anything, but now she's fair game.

"That's disgusting!" I blurt.

"What?"

"You're picking out all the blue cheese!"

"Oh, would you like more blue cheese?" she stabs some globs. "If you wanted more blue cheese, why didn't you say so?"

And yet, and yet . . .

Walking through the woods last summer, we decide to take a shortcut through a bog. Twenty minutes into it my sister and I realize we've made a terrible mistake. Phragmites grass, ten feet tall, has enveloped us. If you stick your arm out, you can't see your hand. There's no turning back because we don't know where back is.

"I can't do it," I whimper.

"Yes you can!"

"Let's just scream."

"No one'll hear us."

"I can't walk another step."

"Come on! Try this!" That's when my sister invents The Way to Walk Through Phragmites. She locks her arm around my waist, then clamps mine around hers. Legs synced like ice skaters, we sweep the stuff down one exhausting step at a time.

"We're never gonna make it." My voice goes wobbly.

She laughs. "If I die first, you can eat me."

We talk almost every day. Although her take on our past is fixed in amber and mine is labile, she's my memory. There are things only we know. It was she who taught me how to tweeze, bunch socks in my bra, touch tongues underwater, make chocolate pudding, smoke and hide the evidence, and sneak brussels sprouts into my underpants during dinner so I could flush them later. When I woke my mother to tell her I'd gotten my period, she said, "Do you know what to do?"

"Yes," I lied, then asked my sister. It was my sister who tried to teach me the facts of life by reading *From Little Acorns* nightly. It was she who beat me up when I howled at the good parts, then kept vigils with me by our bedroom window, waiting for the woman across the alley to take her nightly shower.

And yet, and yet . . .

Do I trust her? Does she trust me? I keep a pound of the coffee she loves in my freezer. "I've got your coffee," I remind her when she calls to say she's coming. Always my sister brings her own can.

I don't know if I could live without her. My eyes flood writing this. Picturing life without my sister is not possible. I love her as much as I love me. *Ma soeur, c'est moi.*

And yet, and yet . . .

We decide to go on a diet. To launch it we leave our husbands and kids behind and head for three nights at a spa. No sooner do we turn into the driveway than my sister is making friends. She makes friends with the doorman, she makes friends with the bellhop, she makes friends with all the waiters and the startled funk aerobics instructor she drags into a corner and thumps her abs at. I hide and I shrivel. I shrink and I pale.

"Why do you have to make friends with everybody?" I whine.

"Why are you so unfriendly?" she laughs.

On the nature hike I'm last; she's first. She scales the ice glen singing. People keep running back down the mountain to check on me: "Are you okay?" "Are you sure you're okay?" At night, after dinner, my sister asks the waiter for two hot-fudge sundaes to take back to our room, where she will simultaneously watch a video and return nine calls from patients. (I'm ambivalent about the phone. She takes hers in the kayak.) Then "What happened?" my sister asks about the movie, and I have to break the spell to fill her in. Then she makes a few more calls and she's ready to turn out the light. Then she wants to talk. Then she wants to sing "Tonight You Belong to Me" in the dark. (I'm melody. She's harmony.) Finally the Volk Girls are ready to sleep.

"Good night, really," we laugh and that's when I hear it. It's the sound my sister has always made at night, a hard swallow that ends with a push of air out through her nose.

Something opens. Something closes. Something opens again.

Open, close, open. It's the sound I fell asleep to the first twelve years of my life in the blue room we shared with organza drapes that met like twin Aunt Jemimas bending over to kiss us, the room I still dream of, the room I still long for, separated by a night table, one arm's length from her, the person Siamesed to my soul, my sister, my half, my beloved Jo Ann.

It was my sister with whom I was bonded so strongly. . . . She was the source of my emotional strength.

QUE SERA, SERA

P. S. BIEL

The voice that poured forth from the voicemail message was that of my sister singing, "Que Sera, Sera." As I rewound and listened again and again, I alternately cried and laughed, trying to do so quietly so as not to arouse the curiosity of my office mates. More than anything, I wanted to figure out how to transport this message home with me. But she'd left it at my office, and this was the last day of a job I was leaving after a mere three months.

The decision to leave was one that I'd struggled with since my second week on the job—a job for which I had relocated to Denver and that quickly revealed itself to be a miserable choice. Meg knew how unhappy I'd been and how conflicted I was about "giving up" so easily. And so once again, my sister—my best friend, my surrogate mother—had known exactly what to say and do to ease me out of my distress.

We came to our relationship a little late in our family life. In looking through early family photos, there are not many to be found of Meg and me together—a few obligatory "big sister holding baby sister" images, but that's about it. She was the oldest of five—three boys and two girls—and I was the second to youngest. With ten years between us, Meg had left for college by the time I turned eight. Aside from not-quite-annual Christmas visits, I didn't spend any significant amount of time with my sister until I was fifteen. That year I traveled to Atlanta to spend my spring break with Meg and her boyfriend (now husband). To say I was nervous about the trip is an understatement: I had never flown before, let alone flown by myself; I hadn't been out of my home state since I was four; and I was worried about how Meg and I would get along. I broke out in hives two days before my scheduled departure—the first, and only, time in my life I have ever had hives.

I needn't have worried. Meg and her husband went out of their way to make me feel welcome and comfortable in their home. They met me at the airport and whisked me off to dinner, spending more on that meal than they normally did for a week's worth of dinners. They filled the remainder of the trip with outings and excursions designed to entertain me. Best of all, Meg treated me like an adult, and we spent hours at home getting to know each other on a level that had never before been possible. She became my idol virtually overnight; she was glamour and independence and success all rolled into one. The trip became an annual event for me, one I continued until moving to Atlanta after college graduation.

During the intervening years, after Mom died when I was eighteen, the bond between my sister and me became forged in steel. While she had always made weekly calls to Mom, I was rarely home to chat with Meg. Now the calls were scheduled around my hours so that she could check on me and my two brothers who were still living at home. Life circumstances dictated that Meg remain in Atlanta with her husband and soon-to-be baby, while finances dictated that I remain in Miami where, between scholarships and tuition breaks, I was able to earn a free ride to the University of Miami.

Over those years, I came to depend upon my sister for the guidance and support that most young adults sought from their parents. Whether for questions about class schedules, career choices, work problems, or boy problems, my sister made herself available to me at all times of day and night. So it was really a non-decision when I chose to move to Atlanta after college. It was hard to say goodbye to my brothers, with whom I'd shared a house for four years. I knew I could count on them in times of need, but it was my sister with whom I was bonded so strongly. She was the source of my emotional strength.

I lived in Atlanta for ten years before venturing farther west, first to Albuquerque and then to Denver. I choose to believe that during those years, while Meg was struggling to raise three children, I returned the favor of support and love that she had shown to me. I would often stop by in the evening just so she could take a shower. Sometimes I stopped by just so she could have a conversation with someone over the age of five. (Her husband traveled extensively when the kids were young.) I tried to make myself available for baby-sitting or running errands or doing dishes. I did so willingly and happily, for I believe this is what sisters do best—we support each other in whatever way is needed. This is certainly what my sister did for me, for not even close to the first or last time, that morning she sang so completely off-key into my voicemail. To this day, I still alternately laugh and cry as I remember that quavering voice singing with such heart, "Que sera, sera, whatever will be, will be. The future's not ours to see, que sera, sera."

We knew we could always count on each other,
and together we were an unbeatable team.

THE KWAN SISTERS

MICHELLE KWAN

Our family has two top-level skaters: me and my sister, Karen, who is two years older than me. Karen finished seventh at the 1997 Nationals in Nashville. Ron likes to joke about "the famous Kwan sisters." He says nobody even knows we have a brother. But we do! We call him Ronald the Great. He's four years older than me, and if he didn't start playing ice hockey when I was five years old, Karen and I might never have gotten into skating.

. . . Karen and I did everything together. We were together on the ice, off the ice, in the morning, in the evening. We were constantly talking in bed, at the rink . . . in the bathroom.

Sometimes we competed at different levels, sometimes at the same level. Karen would take a skating test and rise to a level higher than me, but pretty soon I'd catch up with her and we'd be even again for a while.

I don't think we've ever really felt competitive toward each other. For one thing, I've always looked up to Karen and admired her. And each of us is a totally unique person. If you look at us today, you can see how different we are.

To start with, we don't look alike. Karen is five-foot-eight and I'm the shorty—five-foot-two. The skaters at our rink used to call me "Little Kwan" and Karen "Big Kwan."

When we were little kids, we often wore matching outfits. But that didn't last long. Karen has always had a really good sense of style and fashion. She likes trendy clothes. With her tall, slender body and long legs, she looks great in everything. Long skirts, miniskirts, all kinds of funky combinations.

She also makes some of her own clothes. She's been known to take something she bought and cut off a sleeve or change the neckline. She's not afraid to try new or wacky things.

I'm short and I can't wear all the clothes Karen does. I gave up trying to dress like her when I was about thirteen. I love clothes as much as she does, but now I have my own style.

My style is more classic and simple than Karen's. Sometimes I like preppy-looking things. Most of all I like clothes that are beautifully made and fit me perfectly. I'm too small for the baggy look—I get lost in those enormous blue jeans. The one area where I go crazy is with lipstick and nail polish. I love trying all kinds of wild colors.

Even though we've trained together all our lives, Karen and I don't skate alike. Karen skates like a ballerina. When we were younger, I used to watch her with those long, elegant legs and graceful arms, and I wished I could get that kind of feeling into my skating.

In the past couple of years, I've worked really hard on my programs. Now I have a reputation as an "artistic" skater, and maybe the differences between us aren't as great as when we were little. Basically I have a more aggressive, more athletic style than Karen.

I'm organized, and I need schedules and discipline. Karen has a more dreamy personality. She has lots of different talents, not just skating. She's really funny and smart, and she has a great eye for design—in architecture, clothes, and pictures.

We have different attitudes about skating too. I've always been very competitive. The first time I skated in the U.S. Senior Nationals, I was twelve years old and I came in sixth. I was unbelievably happy that night. But afterward all I could think about was how to do better next year. In 1996 Karen finished fifth in the Nationals. Afterward she told me that she felt lucky to have done so well. She was really happy with that fifth.

I try hard to have that perspective. But I can't help thinking, just a little more effort and I'll do even better. I'm an extremely competitive person—above all, with myself.

When we were kids, Karen was very feminine. I was more of a tomboy. I liked to play really fierce games like handball and dodgeball. In dodgeball, which I loved, I was always the last one standing.

Karen and I are different all right, but we know each other through and through. I swear I can always tell what she's thinking. She's away at college now, and she seems to know when I'm going to call her. If she goes out, she'll leave a message for me on her answering machine: "If this is you, Michelle . . ."

We also know everything about each other's skating. When we were little we knew each other's programs inside out. (We still do.) If Karen skated right before me in a competition, I couldn't watch her because I had to concentrate on my own program. But I could hear her music and the audience. I knew where all the hardest jumps were, so if I heard clapping at that place in the music, I knew she was doing well.

If I skated before her, I could watch her program. That's almost harder than doing the skating myself. There's nothing I can do to help her, and I hate that. My parents have to go through this with both of us all the time! It's torture. My heart just freezes. I grit my teeth. But if she does well, I'm as happy for her as I would be for myself.

Karen has always been my closest buddy and my best supporter. She's been a big part of my success. She's helped me with all three parts of "Work hard, be yourself, and have fun." Without Karen around all the time, it would have taken me a lot longer to know who "myself" really was.

We knew we could always count on each other, and together we were an unbeatable team. But as we got older, the stakes got higher and the competitions got tougher. Then we needed to be able to stand on our own, too, and know exactly who we were.

Sisters who have grown up close to one another know how their daydreams have been interwoven with their life experiences.
—MARGARET MEAD

CABBAGE PATCH STUDENTS

MELINDA RATHJEN

My first teacher was eight years old. My older sister Angela would assemble her "students"—some Cabbage Patch Kids, some stuffed animals, and me—in the basement for "school." Our classes went something like this.

I blurted out an answer to one of the math problems my sister had written on the chalkboard. She insisted, "You have to raise your hand, then I'll call on you!"

I lifted my hand.

"Yes, Melinda?"

"Four," I answered triumphantly.

"Yes, Melinda, that's right. Now, what about this one, class?" Angela pointed to a second addition problem on the board.

The dolls, bears, and stuffed dogs were silent. None of them knew the answer. I bit my lip—neither did I.

The red-haired doll had apparently been holding out on the class, because she now raised her hand—or rather, Angela raised the doll's arm—and squeaked out the answer in a high-pitched version of my sister's voice.

"That's right, good job. Time for recess, class."

We would run upstairs, where we would find a snack and our toddler brother, who was just starting to be fun to play with. When he wasn't stealing toys and attention from us, that is.

School was our favorite game to play, and my sister was always the teacher. Angela had things to teach us. We played with obsolete textbooks our mom had given us, working out math problems on the board. Angela insisted that I raise my hand and wait to be called on, just like the other "students." The Cabbage Patch Kids and stuffed bears, dogs, and cats needed assistance with the chalk and spoke in voices suspiciously like our own. But it felt like they were learning to write, to add and subtract, and to read right alongside me. I was undoubtedly the teacher's pet, except when a cat wandered into class: the cats may have been cuter, but I did better on the tests.

It seemed like play at the time, but I really worked to understand what Angela was showing me. She was three years ahead of me in school and always tried to teach me math on her level. My sister wanted me to learn what she knew, and she took for granted that, with a little help from her, I could learn concepts I wouldn't be taught in school for two more years. Some of my success in school and confidence in my own academic abilities grew out of those lessons; I wonder if her passion for teaching began there in our basement as well. Whatever the reasons were that we played school so much—our family history of professional educators or our delight in playing with school supplies—both of us were shaped by the experience.

Our roles as teacher and student didn't cease when we stopped playing school. Angela continued to teach me things, often without knowing it. In high school, she taught me how to get away with small crimes like breaking curfew, and how to persuade our parents of the things I "needed." She helped me with my makeup and hair for school dances, since I was a tomboy and clueless about such things. I remember the hours just before my sophomore homecoming dance when she insisted on helping me get ready. I sat in a desk chair in our bathroom while she curled my hair and helped me put on makeup. She didn't make fun of my lack of experience in those areas. She just patiently helped me and took pride in the outcome.

We didn't always get along. I learned from her how siblings fight, with slamming doors and foul moods forgotten within a day. Though our sibling snobbery was nearly constant, we knew we would defend each other, if needed. I learned the hard way how to allow others their privacy, even when what they were doing seemed interesting to me, and when it seemed unfair to be left out.

Of course, I was not grateful for these lessons as I was learning them. As surely as she was the older, wiser sister, I was the younger, and I believed, wiser sister. Her mistakes were there for me to learn from and avoid, free to make my own. She won my little brother and me privileges for which we were invariably ungrateful. She let us know that if she hadn't paved the way for us, we would never have had it so good.

I still don't give her firstborn sufferings that much credit, but I do appreciate now, at twenty-three, what an advantage I had in having her as an older sister to teach and encourage me. Angela continues to be a source of encouragement and inspiration, having found success as a sixth-grade teacher. Her classroom now includes real students, and the talent she was born with has grown with each year. I am proud of her.

My sister was more than just a playmate when we were small, more than just an eye-rolling teenage sibling, and more than just a roommate for most of our lives. She has been a source of advice, knowledge, and wisdom. Even when I forget to raise my hand.

*Our sisters hold up our mirrors: our images
of who we are and of who we can dare to become.*
—ELIZABETH FISHEL

SISTERS

LISA GRUNWALD

It came to my sister last summer, in a burst of clarity. We were looking at photographs from summers long gone, when our parents had rented a beach house with cabins for bunking all three of the kids: my brother, my sister, and me. There were the two of us, Mandy and I, dressed alike at six and eight, eight and ten, ten and twelve—in a spectrum of matching Danskin shirts and shorts.

"We dressed ourselves," Mandy told me.

"Of course," I said.

She shook her head. "You don't get it," she said. "We dressed ourselves in the cabins. Mommy was in the main house. We picked out our clothes."

"Oh my God," I said. "You mean . . ."

"I mean," she said grimly, "that nobody forced us to look like this."

Through all the years that we'd bitterly raged at the fact that our mother had dressed us alike, it had never occurred to either of us that we'd been her accomplices. We had imagined that we'd wanted our separate styles. We were sisters, after all, which meant that we ached to be different as much as alike.

I suppose there are sisters who don't compete. I have never met one. Sisters are linked by their sex and their sameness, by being called "the girls," "the daughters."

How can you be a sister and not know how else you might have been? Mandy was smart, but was she smarter? I was funny, but was I funnier? I was younger. She was older. Braver. Taller. Meaner. Stronger. Sisterhood carries with it a sometimes screaming, usually silent "er," the "er" of relentless comparison.

This is not new. From Genesis: "And when Rachel saw that she bare Jacob no children, Rachel envied her sister." From *King Lear*: "He always loved our sister most." From Rudyard Kipling: "Never praise a sister to a sister." From *Hannah, and Her Sisters*: "You're always putting me down." Where in film, life, or literature is an example of sisters who don't take turns being yardstick, speedometer, mirror?

I remember the first outfit Mandy had that I didn't own in a smaller size. It was a brown leather miniskirt with a beige ruffled shirt and a long brown and beige silk scarf as a belt. For an entire fall—the fall she turned fifteen—Mandy wore this on every occasion that she wished to separate herself from me. By the end of that winter, the ruffles had wilted and the leather had stretched hopelessly out of shape.

But we grew into our differences, actually fought to discover them, one by one. The similarities had come first. Apart from the clothes we wore, we did look alike: same long brown hair, same wire-frame glasses, same awful posture, same rampant eyebrows. We sounded alike—so alike, in fact, that we reveled in our ability to fool each other's friends on the phone. We went to the same school and dressed in the same school uniforms. We shared a drawer of navy blue knee socks, battling, at least weekly, over the pair with the better elastic. We shared a bedroom for sixteen years, with two small beds, two small desks, two small shelves for books.

She was my protector, my lookout, my voice at the drugstore counter when I was too shy to ask for help. She killed the spiders, led the way home, rang the doorbells for trick-or-treat. She grew up bold, with a secret shyness. I grew up shy, with a secret boldness. I was sixteen when she left for college. I still remember the grief I felt.

We overlapped for two years at Harvard. She had persuaded me that the school was so large that no one would ever compare me to her. My freshman week, I strolled through the haunted stacks of Widener Library, reveling in their vastness and my anonymity. A woman approached me, an English professor. "You must be Mandy's sister," she said. I stared at her, disbelieving. But she was right. I had to be Mandy's sister.

She'd already started to have her own image: popular, vibrant, overworked, the only Mandy anyone knew. I sat in cafés and wrote dark poems. So I became Mandy's sister again, as I'd always been, except when we two were alone. Alone, she knew that I wanted more than anything to be a writer. I knew that she wanted, more than anything, to know what she wanted to be. In our private constellation, she felt that my star was brighter.

Our mother died when we were twenty-one and twenty-three. We eyed each other hopefully for signs that we could fill in the awful gap for each other. We couldn't. We were sisters, comrades, competitors, peers. We had nurtured our strengths in each other's full view; that left little hope of magic. But we knew we had come from the same woman, and we knew we'd been gypped in the same way.

We lived in the same apartment building—I alone in a studio, she alone with a bad boyfriend. They broke up, and she moved three floors up. I moved, too, my great stroke of independence, to a walk-up all the way . . . across the street. At night, I would go to sleep under the seeming gaze of her twin lighted windows.

In our twenties, I published two novels, and for a while she became Lisa's sister. Then I got married and had a child, and she became Stephen's sister-in-law, Elizabeth's aunt. She moved from New York City to Washington, D.C., and I couldn't help feeling betrayed. For a time, the differences in our lives overwhelmed and severed our closeness. She had ketchup and baking soda and champagne in her refrigerator. I had applesauce and formula in mine. She rarely called. I had something she wanted, and we were both oddly embarrassed by this.

Then a few years ago, she silenced Ted Koppel on *Nightline* with the same look I'd first seen at the age of four, when we shared a bath and I used the shampoo first. She helped elect Clinton, helped change history. I walked down a street with her and gaped when strangers stopped her. I became Mandy's sister again. But now she calls every morning to talk to her niece. She tells me her niece needs a sister.

Sisterhood is to friendship what an arranged marriage is to romance. You are thrown together for life, no questions asked (until later), no chance of escape. And if you're lucky, you find love despite the confinement.

Sisters is probably the most competitive relationship within the family, but once the sisters are grown, it becomes the strongest relationship.

−MARGARET MEAD

THE SHADOW OF THE MOUNTAIN

JOAN WICKERSHAM

*S*ome of the worst fights I've ever had with her have been about writing.

New York, 1985 We meet for a late dinner in a delicatessen. It happens that on this particular night we're both wildly happy. She is newly engaged and has brought her fiancé along, and they're grinning at each other and at me and tangling their fingers together on the black Formica tabletop. I've spent the afternoon with a William Morris agent who has just agreed to take on my screenplay (just so you know: nothing came of it. That's the punch line of so many writing anecdotes: Nothing came of it).

We're drinking beer, talking and joking, laughing and laughing and laughing. And she says, "I have this great idea—I'm going to write a novel about Ahma."

And I blurt out, "But I want to write a novel about Ahma."

Silence.

Ahma was our father's mother. Born in Germany, she rebelled against her family by becoming a dancer, rebelled again by marrying a dancer, came to America because she hated the Nazis, divorced her husband and became a physical therapist for dancers. She lived to be eighty-one, and by the time she died, she was running a movement institute in New York, passing along her methods to scores of dancers and physical therapists.

"Well," says my sister, "then I guess we'll both write novels about Ahma."

"We can't both."

More silence.

I suggest that she could do a biography of Ahma and I could do a novel. (Here, you take this toy and let me play with that one . . .)

Her fiancé, who up until now has stayed out of it, says to me: "She can write about whatever she wants. It's not your birthright, you know."

His words sting, make me recoil. It's like the preliminary rattle of the snake: a warning. My sister has an advocate. It's not just me and her alone anymore, working things out in our own cryptic way. She has someone on her side, who doesn't accept the justice of my taking whatever I want and letting her take whatever's left over.

I go away from this dinner feeling shaken, and ashamed. How would I feel if someone told me what I could and couldn't write? But still there's a part of me that insists on the validity of my outburst, irrational though it was. I know I'm crazy to insist that our both wanting to be writers is a big deal, but she is crazy to insist that it's not. A few weeks later I bring it up with her again. I say:

"I've been thinking, and I had no right to say any of that to you. You should go ahead and write whatever you want to write."

"I don't want to talk about it," she says.

"No, no, listen, we should both write whatever we want, but we need to admit that this is going to be a tough thing for us." I need her to acknowledge that terrible landscape which for one instant was illuminated by lightning—it is ugly and irrational, but it's there and we both saw it.

"I don't want to talk about it," she says again.

And we never have.

I knew very early on that I wanted to write. I did all the usual child-writer things: wrote books which I illustrated and bound between construction-paper covers, banged out short stories on the typewriter my parents gave me for eighth-grade graduation, edited high school literary magazines, won writing prizes. At fifteen I was overjoyed to get a "good" rejection letter from the *Atlantic*—the kind that said, "Sorry, we don't want this story, but we'd like to see more of your work." (Nothing came of it.) I sent some stories to a publisher; and he wrote back that they were good student stories, but I needed to wait until I had something to say.

Fine. But what was I to do in the meantime? Most of my college friends were going on to graduate school in law, or medicine, or psychology. I believed that for me, training for a real career in something other than writing would be tantamount to accepting defeat. But neither did I want to go to a graduate fiction program—I was afraid of being told that I wasn't good enough and afraid that a formal program might teach me writing "tricks" which I would then have to spend years trying to unlearn. So I supported myself with a series of jobs, all of which involved writing, but not the kind of writing I wanted to do. I did newsletters and press releases for a bank, alumni publications for an art school, copywriting for a series of ad agencies.

All the while I kept writing stories and sending them out and getting rejection letters. Every couple of years I would take the law boards and then decide that no, I should hold out a little longer. Sometimes I thought of that scene in *The African Queen* when Katharine Hepburn and Humphrey Bogart get stuck in the weeds and lie down convinced they're going to die, and the camera pulls back to show what they can't see: open water just a few feet away.

But sometimes I thought of misers who hoard all their lives only to discover in old age that the currency has become worthless.

For someone who had declared herself a writer at the age of seven, I was turning out to be a very late bloomer, if, in fact, I bloomed at all.

My sister, three years younger than I, came to writing slowly, sideways. As a child she was interested in archaeology. Then she wanted to be a teacher. Then to run a bookstore, or some other kind of business.

When she got out of college she worked at a publishing house. Then a company that produced corporate publications. Then a book club. She was dancing around the idea of writing, not yet ready to declare her true inclination, even to herself. Or maybe I'm wrong. Maybe she knew all along that she wanted to write, but she was hoping to find some other related occupation that would scratch the same itch. Was she afraid of what I might say? *We can't both.*

. . . But once she chose, once she knew that writing was what she wanted to do, she was fearless. Shortly after that New York deli dinner, she went to journalism school. She sent out queries, followed them up with phone calls, got assignments. Her first published piece came out in the *Nation*. She had a "Hers" column in the *New York Times*. She wrote book reviews for newspapers around the country. She published a book about the myths of motherhood versus the reality, and then another book which was a painfully honest account of three highly educated women trying to adjust to the changes motherhood had wreaked in their lives and in their marriages. Recently I got a chance to fool around with a Nexis database and I looked her up. She had forty-six articles in various publications, some of them pieces she'd written, some of them reviews of her books. What impressed me wasn't just the quantity of her writing, or the quality—it was the quiet, no-nonsense way she'd gone about making a career. She believed her experience in publishing had toughened her up; she had seen the people behind the rejection letters and didn't have to be afraid anymore.

She tried to toughen me up too. Rejection letters flattened me, and I would call her wanting sympathy. She gave it up to a point, but her general reaction was brisk and practical. "So that editor's a jerk," she would say. "Send it out again."

"But what if I really do stink?"

"Joan," she would say.

"But—"

"JOAN!"

She had no patience, either, for long discussions about which magazine or which editor I should try next. Her theory was: it's a crapshoot, a matter of catching the right editor in the right mood on the right day, so there's no point in agonizing about it.

Sometimes I would call complaining that I couldn't seem to finish any of my stories.

"What are you reading these days?" she would ask.

"*Anna Karenina.*"

"And what before that?"

"*Emma.*"

"Well, then."

"Well what?"

"Of course you're depressed. Why don't you do yourself a favor and read some junk?"

One Christmas she gave me a book called *Overcoming Writer's Block.*

"Did you read it yet?" she asked.

"I have a block about reading it."

Did it bother me that she, the younger one, was finding a success that had so far eluded me? If you had asked me to define my worst nightmare, in the early days when all our writing was in the future, when the tension was all about what we might want to write someday, it would have been this: she succeeds and I fail. Yet when that did turn out to be the scenario, for a few years, it wasn't as bad as I might have expected. For one thing, I could not have anticipated the pleasure I would get from reading her work; the very thing I dreaded—that her sensibility might be similar to mine—made her a writer I would have loved reading even if she hadn't been my sister. And her early success, by effectively reversing our birth order, was oddly liberating. I didn't have to feel guilty about the natural advantages of having been born first; for the first time in our lives, I was following in her footsteps. I didn't have to continually look over my shoulder, because there was no one behind me.

There was some friction between us because I wanted her to look at my short stories and offer criticism, and she didn't feel able to do it. Partly, she said, it was because I sometimes used people and events she recognized in my stories, and it was hard for her to be objective about them. And partly it was because she just wasn't that crazy about short stories.

"Well, damn it," I said, "you're my sister and you've been an editor and can't you overcome your aversion for half an hour and help me out?"

I wanted to be where she was, in the safe lamplit room, instead of outside peering in. I admired her courage and wanted her to teach it to me. Now I'm ashamed at having wanted so much. Yes, she was tough and practical—but I think I denied the effort that went into her toughness. When you're trying to be brave and sensible, the last thing you want is someone continually voicing fears that you'd prefer not to consider.

Yet despite the difficulties she was an important teacher for me. Patiently, repeatedly, without ever saying the words but rather by her own example, she imparted the only really worthwhile message a writing teacher can give: shut up and write.

1991 We are entering our thirties. She is well launched as a writer, and I am finally getting off the ground, with several published short stories and a contract for a novel. Now we spend hours on the phone talking shop: agents, editors, publicity, revisions. These days her tough irreverence about the whole publishing process, rather than making me wistful, is bracing. She makes me feel that the two of us can do anything.

The minefield is quiet; grass has grown up. But the mines are still buried, still active.

She asks to read a draft of my novel, and I send it off to her. She calls me, in tears.

"What is it?" I ask. "What is it?"

"It's that conversation I had with Daddy," she says. "You put it in your book. That was private."

I know the scene she means: a sister telling a brother about a disturbing talk she had with their father. "But I changed it."

"Well, you need to take it out."

"But it's not like I wrote a scene where the father and daughter are actually having that conversation. I was writing about what happened between you and me, when you told me about your talk with Daddy and it made me realize we saw him differently."

"I told it to you because I trusted you."

I am silent for a moment. Our father died only a few months before, with brutal suddenness; we are both dazed and raw, and we've told each other a lot of very personal stuff. This is a fight about betrayal. But is the betrayal personal or literary? Is it that I've broken a confidence, or that I've stolen her material? It's both. It doesn't matter. If she's this upset, I'm taking the scene out.

I tell her I'll take it out, but she's too distraught for the concession to make any difference. "I just don't know if I can trust you anymore," she is saying.

Rage. What a ridiculous overreaction. Of course she can trust me. I'll never do it again.

But maybe she can't trust me, since I'm still not entirely sure what it is I've done. Writerly etiquette: you never steal a story from another writer.

But what if the other writer is your sister, the story is about your family, and the two of you have talked so much you're no longer sure where your perspective ends and hers begins?

That is where the tension is between us. That is the green field where the explosions happen. It is not competition, precisely. It's not wanting to do better than she, or get more recognition. It's a struggle over territory: Who does this belong to? Who has a right to this material?

You have to share, says the wise inner voice. There's more than enough to go around.

But no, there isn't. There never is.

That's why, I think, so many horrible arguments seem to erupt over wills. I know of three different families where the siblings have stopped speaking to each other, and all the rifts have to do with inheritance. Either the parents left the property evenly and the poorer children resented it, or the parents tried to equalize things by leaving the poorer kids more, and the richer siblings felt neglected.

In a family with two writers, the legacy comes down to material. There are family stories I want to tell, and I assume she wants to tell them too. So in a sense, although it's unspoken, we're engaged in a race. Those stories will belong to whoever tells them first.

But I don't want to be forever locked with her in some mad battle for the Pole. (If Scott and Amundsen had been brothers, would the wise voice have said to them, Now, now, boys, the South Pole isn't going anywhere and there's enough of it to go around, what difference does it make who gets there first?)

The exploration metaphor isn't as facetious as it sounds, because that, after all, is what writing is—a process of exploration. When you begin working on a piece you know something of what you want to say, but you can't know everything. It's the sense of venturing into new territory that keeps you going. You must feel that the place is open and unexplored. You have to be free to surprise yourself.

When Edward Whymper was attempting to scale the Matterhorn in 1865, an Italian party was assaulting the mountain by a different route. They were just beneath the summit, perhaps a few hours' climb away, when they looked up and saw that the Swiss had already reached the top. So although they had been planning for years, climbing for days, the Italians turned back.

A mountain doesn't belong to anyone. It's nobody's birthright. But the people who grow up in its shadow dream of climbing it. And it happens that my sister and I grew up in the shadow of the same mountain.

And I know, I know. We're not talking about the South Pole here. We're not talking about the Matterhorn. The struggle for territory always looks silly and self-important to those not engaged in it. I watch my cat crouched in the driveway furiously staring down another cat who has dared to venture onto the asphalt; and I think, my God, you guys, get a grip on yourselves, it's only a driveway.

There is something shameful in these reflections. They deny the infinite variety of human experience. As my sister has so often reminded me, I am not her and she is not me. We see the world differently, and we are not the same writer.

Here is an example: She and I both spent the two years before high school in the same bizarre and fascinating place, as girl day students at a boarding school for dyslexic boys. There was one other girl in the school when I went there; when she was there it was slightly more coeducational, with five girls. I've always wanted to write about this experience, but as it happened, she got there first. There's a long section about the school in her most recent book. She told about being called upon in class to give "the female point of view"; she told of the humiliation of being asked by boys whether she wore a bra or used tampons. For her the experience was political; being at that school made her, at the age of twelve, a feminist. I was fascinated to read what she'd written; we had never really talked about the school, and I admired the clarity of her thinking. She had taken raw experience and made it mean something. Seeing it in print, though, made me realize that what it meant to her was different from what it had meant to me. When I think back on that school, I remember the loneliness of it—the other girl who was my friend only because neither of us had another choice, the teachers who were remote and stern and called us by our last names, the dark spruce trees, the frozen pond, the mournful Victorian air of the place. My memories are anecdotal, emotional; I'd like to write about them someday, and her having written her version does not close off the territory.

For a moment I can see quite clearly that there's plenty of South Pole to go around.

1993 My first novel has just come out. I call my sister almost every day and she counsels patience: reviews will come, people will read it, readers will "get" it. It's a good book; why am I such a wreck?

I bristle at her cool tone. Doesn't she understand that I need my hand held? And we have another fight: I am holding your hand, she says impatiently, but you want me to hold it your way. You can't make up a script in your head and expect me to follow it.

Well. She arranges for me to do a reading at the Chicago bookstore where she works part-time. I fly out there still feeling miffed and haughty. When I arrive I find out that she's been sending notes to book review editors all over the country, telling them about my book.

"Why didn't you tell me?" I cry.

She shrugs.

The night of the reading, she stands up at the podium and introduces me. She makes extravagant comparisons to books and authors she loves; the things she says about my book are better than the dream reviews I compose in my head when I'm falling asleep at night. I stand up, and before I start to read she smiles at me, a huge, happy, holding-nothing-back kind of smile. . . .

What remains between us, the last fence dividing my garden from hers, is the question of genre. That is how we've split the territory: I've written fiction, and she's written nonfiction. So far. But lately the boundaries have begun to blur. I'm writing this essay. And a few days ago she called me to broach, in an offhand, self-deprecating way, the idea for a novel she might want to write. "What do you think?" she wanted to know—asking for my opinion, but perhaps, also, for my permission.

"I think it sounds great," I said. "Exactly like the kind of book I'd want to read."

Somewhat to my surprise, I meant it.

Writing this essay, turning these thoughts over and exposing them to the light, has been tremendously calming. And that's the other reason I've come to feel so strongly that we both have to write whatever we want—writing is catharsis. You're trying to find the universal chords in anecdotal experience, but you're also working out what's bothering you; and neither of us can do it honestly with someone else breathing down our necks.

On the other hand, because we love each other, she and I will always be yoked together. As egregious as it is to have to keep asking permission, it's more important for me not to do anything that might hurt her.

So that's where we are. Writing is an anxious, greedy, furtive, solitary undertaking. It is jealous. It is competitive.

And we are both in it. We're in it together.

Chance made us sisters, hearts made us friends.
–AUTHOR UNKNOWN

SISTERS BY LOVE

HELEN E. HADDEN

On November 18, 1960, my mother gave birth to my sister. I was twelve years old. My mother came home from the hospital, but Tina had to stay an extra day. Because of her blood type, they wanted to make sure there were no problems. I went with my aunt and uncle to pick her up the next day. I remember being excited and not really knowing what to expect. I had been around babies before—cousins and friends of my mother's. But this baby was going to be special. She was going to be mine. When my aunt handed her to me when we were on our way home, I was very careful. And when I looked down into that precious little face, I knew that we would always be more than sisters. We would be soul mates.

While most girls my age would have resented having a baby around, I was just the opposite. When she would wake up crying at night, I would beat my mother into her room so I could feed her and change her diaper. I learned to bathe her and dress her. And that first Christmas was the most special of all. I held Tina in my arms and showed her the lights on the tree. I kissed that tiny little face and told her she was my angel.

Some of my friends didn't understand why I didn't want to spend time away from home. They thought that I would want time away from tending to a baby once in a while. And I'm sure they got tired of hearing about Tina all the time.

As she grew older, she became more attached to me. She cried when I went to school or if I went someplace that she couldn't go. When I took her to church, she would not stay in her class. She cried for me. One year I went to summer camp and she cried so much that she got sick.

Things weren't always easy with Tina; she could be a little pest at times. One day she hit me with a hairbrush and I threw a coloring book at her and knocked a front tooth out. It was just a baby tooth, but she cried like someone was killing her, and I got in trouble.

One day when she was misbehaving, I told her that there were leprechauns under the couch. She jumped in a chair and begged me to hold her and promised me she would be good from then on. That didn't last for long when she figured out that there was no leprechauns under the couch.

During her teenage years when Tina hit the rebellious age, I was the only one she would talk to. By that time, I had two daughters of my own. Tina is crazy about them and she spoiled them as much as I had spoiled her. And my daughters are crazy about their aunt.

When Tina married, I sang at her wedding. I bought her bridal bouquet and stayed up all night making birdseed bags. Now she has a son, Jonathan, who is sixteen, and a daughter, Shelby, who's ten. Needless to say, they are as near and dear to me as grandchildren.

Time goes on and some things change while others stay the same. We lost our grandparents and several other family members that were dear to us. Our mother is getting on in years and her health is not good. But I know when the time comes, we will handle it together.

One of the most devastating things I have ever gone through was when the doctor told my sister, in the summer of 2001, that she had cervical cancer. When Tina called me to tell me what the doctor had said, I felt as though someone had ripped my heart out of my chest. I couldn't stop crying: I cried myself to sleep. I cried when I was awake. I cried when I was driving.

And I prayed for God to heal her. I started praying, and I didn't stop. I prayed for healing, of course. I even prayed for God to take this terrible burden from my sister and give it to me. After all, I am older and my children are grown. She still had young children to raise. I just could not get my mind around the fact that I might lose her. But all the while, I just couldn't turn loose and let God handle it.

One day, it was as if God spoke to me and said, "Why are you praying for a miracle, when you won't let go of the prayer?" At that moment, I stopped crying. I prayed another prayer for my sister and one to help me endure whatever was to come. I can't say that I didn't think about it. But I had a peace within me like I had never known. I knew that no matter what, God was in control.

When Tina had her surgery, the doctor discovered that she didn't have cancer after all. Instead she had a hysterectomy and all of the tests returned normal.

Some people might think that there had never been cancer at all. The doctor said there must have been a mistake with the diagnosis. I realize that modern medicine is wonderful and the ability to treat an illness has come a long way. But I also remember the peace I felt after praying to God. I learned a lot from God during that time.

Tina and I are actually half sisters. We have the same mother but different fathers. I was never close to my dad, and she never knew hers. But I've never thought of her as a half sister and neither has she. Blood didn't make us sisters. Love did.

*Even in the orphanage, a sister's shattered spirit
had room to comfort another.*

LILLIAN

JULIA SCULLY

They've cut my sister's hair. But she isn't upset; she doesn't even mention it.

Lillian is in Cottage 24 too. She doesn't sleep in the same room as I do, but I see her every day. I'm glad my sister is here. That is, I would be if I thought about it. But, of course, I don't. Why would I? She's always been there.

Mrs. Gans and Dr. Langer, the director, always call us "the Silverman girls," as if we were the same person. I don't mind. Because usually they're saying, "The Silverman girls are no trouble." We're quiet, do our chores, and never try to run away like Marvin, "the Snake," does, escaping only a few blocks down Ocean Avenue before Dr. Langer in his old black car catches up with him. And we never snip off all the tufts on our chenille bedspreads, as Ada Fleischman did.

We don't talk about the way it was before, Lillian and I, or about Mother, or about when Mother is going to send for us and when we'll be going to Alaska. Or about anything else. As far as I can tell, my sister doesn't talk to anyone. And it seems like nothing matters to her—even that they cut off her hair. It's thick and kinky, my sister's hair, and Mother used to braid it sometimes or else pull it back away from her face with an elastic ribbon and it looked pretty. But now it's short and sticks out in two dark triangles behind her ears.

And it doesn't matter to her that Henry Richmond and Joe Tarver, the big boys in Cottage 24, call her "duck," because they say she waddles. Lillian doesn't even seem to hear them. It's as if she isn't there. That's how it seems to me now, in memory, that my sister wasn't really there. Because if she had been, she would remember some of the things that happened to her while we were in Homewood—which she doesn't. Not even the time she spilled the milk.

It occurs one day when we're all having lunch in the dining room—it's Saturday, so there are tablecloths, and Lillian, like the rest of us, is dressed up, wearing the maroon taffeta dirndl dress that Mother had bought her, the one she used to wear on Sundays when we all went out to Golden Gate Park. She's wearing that taffeta dirndl dress with patent leather shoes, and she's carrying four pitchers of milk into the dining room. That's her job, to help serve the meals.

She's carrying the pitchers by their handles, two in each hand, as she always does, but this time she slips in the middle of the dining room, right in the middle, among the four tables. She lands on her rear end, sits with her legs spread out and milk dripping from her hair and down over her glasses and onto her taffeta dress.

And everybody is laughing at her. Everybody except me. Laughing at my sister sitting on the floor, with the milk dripping all over her, dripping off her thick hair and down the beautiful taffeta dress that Mother had bought for her. But Lillian isn't crying; she isn't even red in the face. She just looks as if she doesn't know what happened.

These are my memories then, of my sister absent, really—not connecting with anyone or anything. And yet, two things make me wonder if my memory lies. One is the photograph—the only photograph of the two of us from that time in Homewood. In the picture, Lillian and I are standing close together; she is caught in the midst of a gesture, she's almost smiling. Her arm is around my shoulder, as if that is where it would naturally be, and I am half turned toward her, almost huddled against her, looking out at the camera from the protective circle of my sister's arm.

The other thing that makes me question my memory of my sister's "absence" is the way she behaves with the little girl, Dorothy. I say "little" because Dorothy seems younger than I, although, as I recall, there were no children younger than I at Homewood. Dorothy doesn't live with us in Cottage 24. And the only time we are with her is on Sundays. That's when most of the kids' parents, their one parent, that is, come to take them out for the afternoon. Only Lillian and I and Dorothy and a few other kids are left at Homewood, kids whose parents are too far away to take them out. Like Freddie, who Mrs. Gans says is a refugee, which means he's German and he doesn't even have a mother or a father, or maybe he does, but nobody knows where they are. Nobody likes Freddie. He gets angry and flushed when he doesn't want to eat something—peanut butter, for instance. But he doesn't have to eat it and he doesn't get punished, either, and that's because he's a "refugee" and his parents are further away than anybody else's, if he has any.

Those of us left on Sunday sit together on the gym steps overlooking the empty playground. And the little girl named Dorothy sits with us there every Sunday. I don't even know what cottage she lives in, but she always wears this dark blue coat with a beautiful dark blue velvet collar. She must have had it from before she was in Homewood, because nobody there has a coat with a velvet collar. Dorothy wears the coat, even though it has worn spots and her arms stick out below the sleeves, because it is from before.

Anyway, on Sunday afternoons we all just sit up there on the gym steps looking out over the empty playground and beyond Homewood's walls to the red tile rooftops. We look at these houses where other kids live and maybe go out in a car with their mother or father and sisters and brothers, and we look out toward the beach, where the Fun House is with the Gypsy lady laughing and laughing all by herself in a glass cage above the entrance. And out beyond that is the ocean.

You can't see the ocean from Homewood, but you know it's out there, because that's where the fog comes from. Rolling in every afternoon, a heavy round curl of fog, stretching from one end of the sky to the other. When it unfolds above you, it turns everything beneath it dark and cold.

And when that happens, little Dorothy starts to cry, crying, it seems, because of the fog. She cries and cries until my sister, who doesn't even appear to be paying attention, slides over next to her, pulls her close, and holds her, until the little girl stops crying.

*Just as it's impossible to point to the very moment one falls
in love, so it was with becoming sisters.*

—ELIZABETH FISHEL

MY SISTER, THE SAINT

PATSY EVANS PITTMAN

I don't know what it was about cleaning up the kitchen after supper that brought out the best—and the worst—in my sister and me. Some days we happily crooned our way through greasy dishes and crusty pans for our family of six. Her pure alto blended with my somewhat reedy soprano as we harmonized on our repertoire of songs—everything from "In the Garden" to "The Whiffenpoof Song."

Other days . . . oh, my, other days. We quarreled and fought. "It's your turn to wash!" "Is not! I washed yesterday!" "You did not!" "Did too!" And at some point, one of us—whoever had won the privilege of drying—would wave the ultimate red flag: "This plate isn't clean." And plop! Back into the soapy water it went.

That's usually when the fussing turned physical. To this day, I hold the name-calling, hair-pulling, face-scratching family championship. Sis, although two years younger, was bigger and stronger; she could have beaten me to a pulp but didn't. She resorted instead to defensive tactics—a gentle push here, a less gentle shove there. I still don't know whether this was due to her innate kindness or fear of reprisal—we shared a bed, and she was a very sound sleeper.

And therein lies another story. My sister was one of those fortunate people who fall asleep as soon as their body reaches a horizontal position. She did indeed sleep soundly, but not soundlessly. Night after night, her rasps and rales kept me awake. And night after night, I elbowed and kicked until finally, exhausted, I fell asleep. If she had bruises the next morning, it was never mentioned.

We couldn't have been more different, my sister and I. She was tall and athletic, with the coppery skin and high cheek bones of our Indian ancestors. I, on the other hand, was short and skinny, "no bigger than a bar of soap after a hard day's washing," my grandfather always said. During summer vacation, Sis went fishing with Dad or played football and baseball with the boys, or, when she was younger, ran off to visit with our neighbor's pigs. I holed up in our dank basement where it was cool, buried in a book. I loved school and words and numbers. For excitement, I studied an old algebra book I found, or figured square roots or diagrammed sentences. It's too bad the word "nerd" hadn't yet been coined—I would have been first in line for the title.

I was a little shy and reserved. Sis had a quick wit and a natural affinity for defusing tense situations. I envied her the quick camaraderie with all kinds of people, especially boys. She got a bra and a boyfriend before I did. Younger sisters aren't allowed to do that, are they? It was unforgivable.

I was probably fifteen and Sis thirteen the summer a really, really cute boy came to stay with our next-door neighbors while his parents traveled. I adored him the minute I saw him and knew in my heart that we were destined to be together. Forever. It was only a matter of time. One day I looked up from my book long enough to see him and my sister in the side yard playing a game of mumblety-peg. The book must not have been too interesting, because I combed my hair, maybe even put on a touch of lipstick, and strolled out into the yard, hoping, knowing, that I would be noticed. I was. "Move," the love of my life ordered. "You're in the way." I was crushed. I vowed then and there that I would never, ever speak to my sister again.

I did, of course, although not always kindly.

It wasn't until we were adults, working in the same office, that my sister told me how much she envied me when we were kids. "I almost hated you," she said. "I dreaded getting a teacher you had had. 'You're Patsy's sister? Oh, such a sweet girl. And so smart.' And on and on and on. It was like I didn't have a name. Just 'Patsy's sister.'"

It was then I realized that each of us, in coveting the gifts of the other, had undervalued our own unique talents.

Growing up is a wonderful thing. We're still different—different from each other and different from how we were as kids, but we've become best friends. I still love words and numbers, and I just finished a sixteen-year term as church treasurer. She leads a women's Bible study, spoils her grandchildren, and makes fantastic special occasion cakes. I was a widow for twelve years, and the running joke between us was that I expected her to make my next wedding cake. Her stock reply was, "By that time, I'll be too old to bake it, and you'll be too old to eat it." But this time, the joke was on her. In April 1996, I did indeed remarry, and she did indeed create a beautiful—and delicious—wedding cake.

My sister is an incurable good-doer, although she sometimes runs face first into that old saying, "No good deed goes unpunished." She befriended an elderly lady in her apartment building who suffered from frequent memory lapses and mental confusion. Pearl asked Sis to make a doctor appointment for her; however, when appointment time rolled around, not only was Pearl not ready to go, she was highly indignant that this presumptuous woman, whoever she was, thought she needed to see a doctor. By the time that "presumptuous woman" got back to her apartment and cancelled the appointment, the phone rang. Pearl was upset; she couldn't understand why her dear friend, who had been so kind in the past, now refused to take her to the doctor.

"Sis," I tease, "You're going to have so many stars in your crown, you won't be able to hold your head up." She just laughs and heads off on her next mission of mercy.

When our father had a stroke, my sister, although still working full-time, did more than her fair share in helping with his care. Often, when she had a day off, she would call. "Don't worry about Daddy today. I'll be there." Those twenty-four hours of freedom were the best gift she could have given me.

Sis has always been a little heavier than she would like, although she carries her weight well and looks great. But did I ever tell her that? Oh, no. From the mouth of a ninety-eight pound weakling came only taunts and insults. During our dishwashing wars, I called her every hurtful name I could think of. Now, it's her turn. In the last ten years or so, I've filled out some. Actually, I've filled out quite a lot. Let me put it this way: I'm no longer a ninety-eight pound weakling. But has Sis ever mentioned this very obvious fact? No, never. Not even once.

That's how I know my sister truly is a saint.

Forever, *Wherever* Sisters

Only a sister shares the secrets of your soul.

SHARING SECRETS

PATRICIA PINGRY

A once heard a family psychologist say that siblings have the closest of all relationships—closer even than that between parent and child. Because siblings have the same parents, the same grandparents, the same ancestors, the genes in each come from the same source. But theories seldom work in life.

The tension between my sister and I began with my birth. She had been the only child for four defining years before I came along, and the sides were chosen at conception. I was born on our father's birthday. Her birthday was four days before our mother's. Katherine favored my mother's family; I looked like my father. On car trips, she sat in the back seat behind the passenger seat, I sat behind the driver. My father always drove.

My birth was, I think, a shock to my parents. They knew I was coming, of course, but they had chosen only a name for a boy, so certain were they of the sex in those days long before ultrasound. The arrival of a daughter stunned them both. They had named their first daughter after her grandmothers and there were, quite literally, no family female names left. What to do about the baby? The hospital asked the name for the birth certificate. Friends and family wanted to know the name. My parents were pressed from all sides.

My four-year-old sister had a new doll, the consolation prize for first-born girls when a new baby comes along. The doll was a popular "Patty Ann" doll which

Katherine loved, certainly more than a newborn rival. So the next time the hospital administration asked for the new baby's name, Katherine had the answer. I was given the doll's name—Patricia Ann—and I became the real-life consolation prize.

My sister and I weren't particularly close growing up. Those four years magnified our different interests in school and created a distance that couldn't be surmounted. Advertisers tell of closeness "like a sister's" but we shared none of that. We'd both read *Little Women* but were not driven to emulate their experiences. Quite the contrary. We spent all of the growing up years trying to distance ourselves from each other—in clothes, interests, colleges. If she liked something, I did not. Then marriage and children brought further personal and geographical distances that we wouldn't attempt to surmount.

Daddy died in autumn. The leaves were blazing red and gold; the chrysanthemums were brilliant. Days and nights in the hospital blurred until we were unable to say how much time had passed. Since he and Mother were no longer married, only Katherine and I were at his side; and by the time it was over, we were both drained. She and I chose gold for the chrysanthemums. Only she and I stood at the graveside as the oaks and maples cast their luminous glow in the late afternoon sun. Only she and I stood lost in the memories of a father who had one mantra: "If you don't like something, change it," yet was unable to transform the alcoholism that shaped his daughters' lives, devastated his marriage, and destroyed his health. The alcoholism was a secret around which we built a sturdy barrier and never shared with friends or even extended family members.

Thirty years later Katherine and I were in another hospital, eating cafeteria food, settling down in plastic-covered armchairs as we waited to see if Mother would survive her third or fourth or maybe fifth heart attack. She'd had so many we'd lost count. Katherine had moved our ninety-four-year-old mother into her house; and she called me when the doctors put Mother on life support. I went as soon as I could get a flight. At the hospital, the doctor pressed us to make a decision about life support and to prepare ourselves for Mother's death. Fortunately, Mother kept writing notes; she was hungry, hadn't eaten for days, and wanted to go home. We promised her she could go soon; but when we were alone, we discussed those decisions the doctor was urging on us.

During the day, we hovered over the hospital bed. At lunch and dinner, we talked about the past. After one lunch, Katherine lit her cigarette, and we reminisced about how, as teenagers, we both had sneaked cigarettes. Like most teenagers, we were convinced that we were keeping our smoking a secret from our parents. As adults, however, we knew that we had fooled only ourselves.

At other times, we talked about the Christmases we had shared, especially the one when Santa brought bicycles to us both. Mother and Daddy loved playing Santa and planned for it all year; but this Christmas, our grandmother gave away the bicycle secret at Thanksgiving dinner. The silence that followed that announcement was tangible but priceless to us girls who hadn't believed in Santa for years. But something magical died at that moment and we both knew it.

In the hospital waiting room, we talked about our marriages and subsequent divorces. We mourned lost chances and regrets that will never be revealed to anyone else. We recalled the time of our marital separations when we trooped back to the small town where we grew up—Katherine with her four children and I with two—and moved in with Mother. For about a year we both tried to maintain the façade that we were only on an extended vacation. But we laughed as we remembered the time when my son had his sister surreptitiously gather dried grass and leaves. Then they used their grandmother's magnifying glass to angle the sun's rays onto the grass until it began to smoke. By the time my daughter became scared and ran to me, screaming, the wooden steps at Mother's backdoor were on fire.

And we spoke of the birth of our children. Soon after my marriage to a lieutenant in the U.S. Army, I took a train for New York and from there, my husband and I were to board a ship for a three-year stay in Germany. The scene at the train station was gloomy. My father seemed to take it hardest and said to me, "If I had known you would go to Germany, I would not have let you get married." Katherine, nine months pregnant, was also very emotional. Only my mother seemed positive. After all, her marriage had taken her far from home. As I hugged them all one by one and boarded the train, I whispered to my sister to please write as soon as the baby came. I was eager to know if it was a girl or a boy. She responded that she and her husband still hadn't determined the names for either a boy or a girl.

We were only a couple of days out of port when I received a telegram from my father. He was a grandfather now, he said, for Katherine had given birth to a baby at almost the very hour I had sailed. She had named her daughter Patricia.

After sixty years of sisterhood, I now know that the psychologist I heard years ago was wrong. It's not genes or inherited traits that make sisters close. It's the secrets they share, collected throughout the life of a family; and these secret memories forge a bond that cannot be breached. Only a sister shares the secrets of your soul.

*Nurturing relationships are what shape who
we are and how we live.*

SATELLITE SISTERS: UnCommon Senses

JULIE DOLAN

We are five real sisters, born of the same parents, raised in the same house, fed the same clam chowder. We shared rooms, took baths, and went to camp and school together. We spent hours outside playing dodgeball, kickball, baseball, football, and capture-the-flag. When it got cold, we moved inside to play school, board games, and make houses out of cardboard boxes, blankets, and stacked furniture.

I am the oldest sister. Liz, Sheila, and Monica follow in quick succession, and Lian is the youngest. We also have two older brothers, Jim and Dick. A younger brother, Brendan, was born among the sisters.

We had one TV, one phone, and one station wagon. If you wanted to watch television, you would have to negotiate with Jim and Dick to watch *The Love Boat* by agreeing to turn to the Yankees game during the commercials. On the phone, you learned to talk quickly and in hushed tones because there was always someone listening or waiting. And if you wanted the station wagon to go shopping in Westport, it meant you had to drop off Brendan and his friends at the movies first.

We wore the same clothes. In the winter, the girls wore matching red coats and red berets; the boys had blue jackets. In spring, we had coordinating Easter dresses. My all-time favorite sister dress was a Marlo Thomas-*That Girl*-like dress—in white with red and blue polka dots. For summer, my mother found six bathing suits—four tank suits for the girls and two Speedo-style racers suits for the boys—all in the same Florence Eisman pattern. Brendan and Lian, as the two youngest of the group, missed out on the initial seasons of many of these outfits but were compensated by having a ten-year supply of the same jackets, dresses, or bathing suits.

You were always someone's younger or older sibling. No matter what you had to do, you could always bring along a brother or sister. My first day of kindergarten was less traumatic because Mrs. Friend asked me if I was Dick's sister. When I went to camp, Liz and Sheila were on the bus with me. Jim drove me to school dances. Monica, Lian, and Sheila helped me look at colleges. Dick moved me three or four times. At my wedding, my brothers and sisters were the ushers and bridesmaids. And, on my first day at a real corporate job, Liz came with me to the employee orientation.

I learned that what happened to others affects me. If Dick got in trouble for carelessly blocking the back door with his discarded hockey bag, my relative standing with my mother was elevated. If Sheila and Monica were fighting about a sweater, I knew that this was not the moment to appeal to my parents about extending my curfew. When Jim and Dick painted me instead of the picnic bench, we were all going to get it.

We honed our sisters' act doing the endless dishes for a family of ten. We didn't think of it as an act then; we were doing what we were told. Night after day after night, we washed, talked, laughed, and did some truly bad renditions of "You Don't Bring Me Flowers." Despite being raised in the era of the Osmonds, the Jacksons, and the Bradys, we harbored no career aspirations in the entertainment field—only the hope that someday our mother would get the dishwasher fixed. In truth, we were more like the Loud family on the original "reality television" series, PBS's *An American Family*: big talkers, bad haircuts, and, well, loud.

Like most family acts, the inevitability of growing up took its toll. We stopped washing dishes together and started living our own lives. We moved out, went to school, got degrees, slept on each other's couches, borrowed money, lent money, got married, got promotions, lost weight, gained weight, stayed single, quit jobs, moved again, had kids, got divorced, found yoga, and stayed friends. It was around this time that we decided to take the plunge and work together.

We discovered that, after years of trying to distinguish ourselves from one another during childhood and adolescence, we wanted to reconnect with each other as adults. We had different lives, and we lived all over the world, but we still needed each other. So we started a public radio show called *Satellite Sisters* to have the kind of conversations on the air that sisters have in real life. We thought that connection might resonate with other people.

Each week, I get up in the middle of the night in Bangkok, down a Coke, and hook up by ISDN line to Liz and Sheila, who are eating lunch in New York, and Lian and Monica, who are drinking their first cups of coffee on the West Coast. Each week we talk, laugh, and sometimes Lian cries. We try to entertain, encourage, empathize with, and enlighten our guests, listeners, and each other.

So far, we've talked about going to a college reunion, clearing bad credit, finding a lump, tracking a lost dog, having sex after childbirth, breaking the glass ceiling, making the perfect pie, surviving a brain tumor, applying to kindergarten, applying to college, living more simply, writing poetry, getting a new roof, and raising trout.

What surprised us when we started talking on the radio was why people said they were listening. They told us that it really didn't matter what the topic was— they just liked listening to sisters talk. People immediately understood what the show was really about—connecting with family and friends.

We didn't have to explain what a Satellite Sister was. Our listeners knew. They wrote to us to tell us about their three sisters, or their one brother who is like a sister, their mothers and grandmothers, their running group, knitting group, scrapbooking group, their book club, their painting class, their college roommates, their best friends, their cubicle mates, and their cul-de-sac neighbors. Sometimes they wrote to us to say that they didn't have any brothers or sisters and liked listening to us because it allowed them to imagine what having a sister might be like. Others wrote to us about being distant or estranged from their sisters and apologized to us for not being close to their family.

They wrote us about monthly dinner groups, weekly girls nights out, spa weekends, and annual week-long reunions. They told us about how they play music, read books, swim, sail, ski, and ride horses together, bareback and naked. They wrote to us about supporting each other through promotions, firings, childbirth, cancer, divorce, relocations, hysterectomies, widowhood, marriage, and raising teenagers.

Our listeners believe what we believe: that being someone's sister, or brother, or teacher, or friend, is what gives meaning to our lives. Nurturing relationships are what shape who we are and how we live. We know that you don't have to have shared the same bathroom or traveled in packs of ten to be connected. Those just happen to be our reasons. Most of us are bound together by sharing the small everyday acts of life with the people in our lives who support, accept, sometimes bust, and always encourage us.

A sense of connection is the realization that going through life with other people is a better way to go. My sisters and brothers give me the courage to try things, back me up when I fail, laugh at me, laugh with me, teach me, occasionally cry with me, and show me how to understand people who are different from me. I don't ever want to live with my brothers and sisters again, but I don't want to live my life without them.

Writing a book with my sisters seems like a natural progression from playing dress-up, riding bikes, and styling each other's hair with the one family blow-dryer. It is just another group activity, like going to swim-team practice or to the library. It is not something that I would ever attempt by myself. Like going to kindergarten, camp, or college, writing a book together with my sisters makes it OK.

Like the radio show, we are working together, alone. This time we are sitting at computers thousands and thousands of miles apart, writing to each other about what we remember about growing up and how growing up in a big family has shaped us as adults. It is a collective look back at life in a big family and the uncommon senses we have developed along the way. We aren't radio professionals. We aren't journalists. We aren't experts. Some of us aren't even writers. We are just sisters. And maybe that is enough.

*No one knows better than a sister how we grew up, and
who our friends, teachers, and favorite toys were.
No one knows better.*

—DALE V. ATKINS

THE SWEETNESS OF SISTERHOOD

DANIELLE GOLDSTEIN

picture captures the earliest recollection. I've stared at it so many times, perhaps memory took hold of my consciousness and etched itself there. We're sitting on a white leather ottoman in my grandparents' living room in Joliet, Illinois. Yellow gingham dress hems give way to chubby legs, and little lacy socks top patent leather shoes. I'm bald except for a few fuzzy tufts, but Julie's long, brown curls hang to her shoulders and frame a perfect three-year-old face. We're clutching stuffed yellow bunnies and looking up into the camera with half grins. It was 1974.

Now that Easter photo is tucked behind a cheap plastic frame and makes up one piece of a refrigerator collage of grocery lists, souvenir magnets, coupons, and other snapshots. Now that we are firmly planted in adulthood and fifteen hundred miles apart, pictures like that one help me recall the memories—those specific events in our shared lives to which I can point and tell with certainty the accompanying story. If only there had been a picture for each day of our lives. If only we could retell day by day the story of that delicate handful of years when we were growing up. If only. I fear that something in the air would be altered permanently, that we would swoon wildly at the sweetness of it all and then collapse under its weighty veil.

It is not the days we remember, anyway, someone wise once said. It is the moments. I suspect that the relationship I share with my older sister is at once similar to that of thousands of other women, and distinctly ours. We were born within two years of one another and are the only children in our family. The result of this familial lottery could only have been produced by some mysterious and powerful genetic concoction. Perhaps when the Human Genome Project maps the gene for intensity, we will understand why we are like we are. But until then, all the nurturing in the world could not modify the emotional, high-strung, moody, overpowering, exquisite relationship my sister and I share to this day. That intensity, I'm convinced, was hard-wired. No person or experience could curb it or make us act differently toward one another. It's as if the rules that applied to other relationships and human beings were simply not going to suffice for us. Our emotion alone would have bent and snapped conventional ways of relating. Somewhere in that genetic hard-wiring, however, is a force that keeps pulling us together when so much of what transpires between and around us ought to pull us apart.

For the first three thousand nights of my life, Julie slept two feet from me. We must have lulled each other to sleep with the sound of our breathing. There must have been a time when we knew each other's nocturnal noises and responded to them in a sister code known only to us. I remember the comfort of having her near during winter nights so long by a child's measure.

The summer was different. My young parents would put us to bed in their room and head over to the neighbors' house for frozen daiquiris at dusk. Their window looked out over the lawn and through the row of skinny evergreen trees; we could make out the stripes on their shirts and the shine of their dark hair. My father's laugh called loudly and spread quickly against a pink wispy sky as he told a joke. My mother's voice did not join in the laughter, but her presence was palpable. When darkness finally fell, we'd settle in under the sheet and play the letter game on each other's backs. I used to try to fool her by tracing out cursive letters. She would antagonize me by putting her arm under my pillow, stealing all the cool spots.

For many years our childhood was marked by the singular position we enjoyed as the only grandchildren on both sides of the family. Our grandparents, however, were not finished raising their own children when we came along. Though we spent weeks with them during the spring and summer, I think my grandparents were still recovering from their parenting roles too much to fully enjoy our presence. Our teenaged aunt and uncle were all too happy to take over babysitting responsibilities. As the youngest of seven, their desire to inflict pain and suffering on somebody younger than themselves was great. Sometimes my sister and I simply endured during those visits. For hours we were forced to stare at the alarm clock until my grandmother returned from her errands (only to find us happily watching TV). Other times, they got a kick out of tying our shoelaces together and sending us for a night hike in the woods behind the house. But those actions were harmless. Looking back, Julie and I were too busy doing the job of children—growing and playing and never stopping the tilt-a-whirl of childhood—to wonder what was to come.

I also suspect that like thousands of other women, nobody but my sister and I understand our relationship. So often others mistake our intensity for a deep-seated dislike of one another. On a recent trip to Colorado to visit my sister and her family, we had to leave the dinner table after a terrible scene from our adolescence was unexpectedly recounted. In her version, I'm chasing her around the figure-eight of our little ranch house in Sheboygan, Wisconsin, with a butcher knife yelling, "I'm going to kill you!"

Shocked and dismayed, I quickly responded with my version in which she is chasing me around the figure-eight of our little ranch house in Sheboygan, yelling,

"I'm going to kill you!" I could not believe she had it so wrong. She could not believe I had it so wrong.

We changed roles many times throughout our adolescence. Our sibling dramas cast each of us as victim and villain. One afternoon, in an attempt to confiscate my favorite sweatshirt, I kicked my foot through the bathroom door. Sometimes we even left scars on each other. I have three on my left hand from Julie's preferred combat technique, scratching. Many times, though, it was neither she nor I who caused the pain. Those physical battles were the result of a much more hurtful battle taking place inside.

I remember the day we officially became adolescents. Only an hour after our parents made the announcement, my father packed a borrowed pickup truck with a new mattress and the rest of his belongings. I realized instantly that the whole conversation had been premeditated. They weren't going to ask us what we thought. They had already decided for us. Julie sat on the floor between our dad's legs, and I leaned on the couch close to our mom. But they were already gone. And so were we.

From that day forward, our parents took a backseat role. With our father out of the house and our mother absent in the way that so many single mothers are forced to be, Julie and I went from playmates to accomplices in becoming. We made the usual teenage forays into the world of rule-breaking and rebellion, and later alcohol, drugs, and sex too. But with such lack of supervision, we were left to decode those adventures ourselves. Suddenly, it was not enough to be a sister. Armed with very few capabilities, we became each other's parent and protector too.

In the presence of our parents, we were a united force powerful enough to withstand any interrogation and wise enough to level any accusation. Alone, we were the object of each other's anger at what had happened to our family. Alone, we multiplied the trials of adolescence just to see how much the other could withstand, just to see who could become chief of our kingdom of two. To have control over the other was to alleviate, if just for a moment, the rage and anger vying for keeps in our once satisfied hearts.

It's difficult to talk about my sister without painful memories, some real and some imagined, making their way into the light. My sister was my witness. She shared my fate. We were born to take those first few precarious steps together—our first play, our first tennis tournament, our first concert. Later it seemed as if we were born to mirror the nips and tears of a messy adolescence. A family surviving instead of thriving. An eating disorder that came to nibble away at the hurt. Identities forged from memories of better days and the grit of persistence. And now?

As adults, nobody (least of all our parents or husbands) can account for our closeness. Still, there are times when the tender little girls from the Easter photo are replaced by evil twins. If we could scratch and hit each other just one more time and not be locked away for it, we would. If we weren't certain Julie's kids could hear us, we would revert to the verbal treacheries we honed as teenagers. And our mother is still on constant alert for the battle to end all battles, the one where someone loses an eye, or worse.

But we resist those temptations and give in, instead, to languorous, detailed telephone conversations at all hours of the day and night. After thirty some years, the primal urge to know how the other spent every moment of her day rises to the surface. We surprise each other with our telepathic ability to purchase the same sweater at the same time in two different states. We are amazed at the insane way our handwriting curls and loops in exactly the same places. We compare wrinkles and spots and marvel at the genetic forces at work. Undoubtedly, there are moments when the weighty veil of that delicate handful of years still tries to smother us. But somewhere there is an open window, and in wafts the sweetness of sisterhood. In that charged air the intensity of two sisters thrives and carries us toward dreams and passion and forgiveness and a desire to renew that most profound relationship that has chosen us.

Do angels really connect long-distance sisters?

DOWN TO EARTH

COLLEEN HUGHES

My baby sister, Shannon, is twenty-eight years old. She has two babies of her own: Hannah, two, and newborn Isabella. Shannon's Hannah and my Louisiana are very close, "best-friend cousins." They have the exact same giant stuffed panda; Hannah calls my daughter Louisi-hannah; and photographs and letters (of sorts) fly back and forth across the thousand miles that separate them. But these cousins, and Shannon and I, don't see each other enough.

The other day I called Shannon to catch up. I expected her usual confident, slightly smart-aleck "Hey, Colleen." Instead, on this particular afternoon, I got a plain old no-nonsense hello.

"Hey, Shan," I said, "what's the matter?"

"Things are a little crazy," she said. While trying to cajole Hannah into eating a few more bites of tuna salad, Shannon was packing the diaper bag for an afternoon of errands. Isabella was squalling. Shannon hadn't slept well because her husband, Les, a doctor, had been on call at the hospital all week. "And it's pouring rain outside," Shannon sighed. "Call me back tonight?"

"I will. And I hope that rain lets up," I said, then hung up and said a prayer for my sister. *She needs some help, God, and I sure wish I could do something. Shannon was strong and capable, but still my baby sister.*

When I had gone off to college, third-grader Shannon and our brother Robbie (in second grade at the time) sent me several letters a week. I was at Louisiana State University in Baton Rouge, only an hour or so away, and I went home most weekends. But Shannon and Robbie were determined to be part of my everyday life, every day. And they were. My dorm room was decorated with their construction paper collages and Popsicle-stick mobiles, Wonder Woman and Star Wars drawings, and letters.

Every once in a while I reread those old letters, the only love letters I've kept to this day. After hanging up with Shannon, I opened my deepest desk drawer and pulled them out from under a pile of pictures of Louisiana. The first few made me laugh till I cried, with Robbie showing off his new vocabulary words: "See me eat meat," and Shannon's own homemade crossword puzzles: "2 down—It comes after one." (The answer was "too.")

Then I opened this one from Shannon, who'd stayed home sick on a school day (I've corrected the spelling for you, just like I always did for her):

Dear Colleen,

I'm bored because Ryan is sleeping. Robbie, Jaime, and Kelly are at school. And Daddy is at work. Ruffles [the dog] is outside, punished. Mom is washing clothes. So I have nothing to do except write to you. So you help a lot. Even if you are far away at college.

Sitting in my house, far away in New York, I wished it were as simple to help my baby sister now. That night I called her back.

"Hey, Colleen," she answered, sounding like herself again. Isabella was sleeping and Hannah was playing with her panda. Everything had worked out fine. "You just caught me at a bad moment," Shannon said. "And that was good. It helped to know you were thinking about me."

"Thinking isn't doing, though, Shan," I said. "I wanted to be there to hold the umbrella while you buckled the kids into the car."

"It was the funniest thing," she said. "The rain stopped just as we stepped out the door."

I told Shannon about the old letter. Angels fly back and forth, I think, carrying love and care in our phone calls and letters and long-distance prayers, connecting sisters who can't spend enough time together, and two-year-old cousins who barely know each other, really. Not yet, but they will. With the help of angels.

You, Edythe, like Maya Angelou has said, are my sister-friend.

CORETTA AND EDYTHE SCOTT

CORETTA SCOTT KING AND EDYTHE SCOTT

My dear sister Coretta,

I am sitting here tonight thinking about us. How close we were as children, sharing everything, doing everything together, always the leaders, always picked for the plays and the concerts because we were talented and attractive. The kind of kids teachers just knew would cooperate. When I went to Antioch before you, I learned about sibling rivalry in one of my courses, and I didn't believe there could be such a thing. We certainly never competed or were jealous—even if you did have more boyfriends. And you've forgiven me for telling you there was no Santa Claus.

Do you remember when you were five, already so physically strong, and you helped me pull the first bucket of water from the well outside of our house? That became a metaphor for our lives. All these years we've pulled each other up, supported each other, and taken care of each other. Even Martin saw that. He called us the twins. He'd be giving a speech in some big auditorium and he'd say, "My wife isn't here tonight. But her sister is in the audience—so if I want to see Coretta, I just look down there at Edythe."

I've never told you this, but Martin comes back to me in my dreams. It's always when we're up against the wall and you don't know what to do. He comes to me smiling and joking and says it's going to be all right. That's when I call you and get very positive and tell you we'll find a way. Sometimes I think we would have been even closer if Martin hadn't died. You were my best friend for so long, but now there are always so many others around you, wanting a piece of you, there isn't always as much room for the two of us.

When we were growing up you always told people you thought I was the smarter one, that I knew everything. But I have learned from you. You've taught me to live each day as fully as I can, because no one knows what tomorrow will bring. You taught me to rely on the spiritual force in the universe, how not to worry or to be afraid. And I hope I've made you laugh and brought some joy into your very serious life.

I was trying to explain to someone what keeps our relationship working and I used that phrase from *The Prophet* by Kahlil Gibran: I said, "We have spaces in our togetherness." Doesn't that describe us well? We've never been the kind to say things; we just do for each other. So, for once, I wanted to tell you how blessed I feel to have a sister that I'm comfortable with and that I like as well as love.

Edythe

Dear Edythe,

Your beautiful letter carried me back to those days when it was more common for us to pick up a pen than a telephone. I particularly remembered a letter you'd written to me when I was in Boston studying music at the New England Conservatory. I hadn't told you that Martin had proposed to me on our first date, several months earlier. Because this was the most important decision I could make in terms my future, I wanted to make it myself, without your influence. I prayed and struggled and then I had a revelation in a dream. I saw Daddy King, Martin's father, smiling at me approvingly. The next morning I woke up with a sense of inner peace that I interpreted to mean the relationship would work out. Right after that, your letter came, as if you'd read my mind. "Don't be silly, girl," you wrote. "You know how difficult it is to find intelligent, stable, well-adjusted men"—a whole string of adjectives. And then you wrote, "You won't have your career as you dreamed it, but you will have your career."

That summer you came to live with me in Boston and we used to play games with Martin on the phone because he couldn't tell us apart. And remember how he wanted to test me on my cooking? You and I prepared this fine dinner for him. We really were old-fashioned girls who knew how to cook. Afterwards he'd tell people, "I asked Coretta to cook a meal for me and she dispatched Edythe. The two of them teamed up on me!"

You've always known instinctively just how to make me comfortable and support me. I will never forget the day after Martin's funeral, when you packed up your son and came to stay with me. The fact that I never had to ask meant so much to me. You just knew ahead of time how deeply I was going to need you and you were there. I will always be grateful for your foresight and your presence. Having you, my sister, in the house for two years with me and as a surrogate mother to my children, especially when I had to be away so often, was a comfort no one else could have provided. And when there were little frictions among my staff, you were always careful to keep negative things away from me so that I wouldn't worry.

I'm so glad you've been with me whenever anything important has happened, although I still regret that you were ill and couldn't come to Oslo for the Nobel Peace Prize. But I have wonderful memories of all the times you traveled with me on special occasions, giving advice and helping me write letters and speeches. Writing was never my forte, but you had that talent back in high school when you were editor of the paper. I always admired that you had such a good mind and a grasp of things. You did so much reading and thinking. I was more an activist kind of child. It seemed to me you always had so much information—you had that way of eavesdropping on the adults—and I loved when you'd tell me things and share the secrets you'd found out.

If you hadn't gone to Antioch College first and made a place for me and pulled me in, I'd have missed having the experience that prepared me for my role today. The emphasis on multiculturalism and the democratic community there were the perfect training for my life's work.

I wish that your teaching commitments at Cheyney State and my busy schedule would allow us to visit more often. When you're around I laugh more, and I need that because I tend to be so serious-minded. You have a way of finding humor in anything. You can pull the theater out of life. Being with you, I can be completely myself. You appreciate the stresses I have being a public figure, meeting people's expectations, fulfilling a role. When it's just us, I can be myself and know you'll love and understand me no matter what. You don't want anything from me except my happiness.

I'm very lucky. I don't have a husband, but I do have a sister. A sister I can talk to about personal things I wouldn't tell anyone else. A sister who does things for me, consoles me, comforts me. A sister with whom I can share my burdens and my joys. It's very hard in this world to find someone who can walk in your shoes, but you come closer to that than anybody. A lot of sisters are not friends. You, Edythe, like Maya Angelou has said, are my sister-friend.

Coretta

You can't think how I depend on you,
and when you're not there, the color goes out of my life . . .
—Virginia Woolf

SISTERS' PACT

Sharon Robertson

Our company's moving and Roger and I both got promoted! Can you believe it? I'm so excited!"

As my older sister, Kelly, told me her good news, I couldn't help laughing. Between her recent engagement to Roger, and now this, I could just picture her jumping up and down at the other end of the phone.

"But wait," she said, "I haven't told you the best part. Both of our new jobs are in—are you ready? San Francisco! We have to leave in a month, so we're going to plan the wedding there. Won't that be great?"

I swallowed hard. "Yeah, swell. I'm really happy for you, Kel," I lied. San Francisco was three thousand miles away.

My sister and I had a deal. We had pledged that when we grew up, we wouldn't move far away from each other. We were going to raise our families together and swap stories about our grown-up kids over afternoon coffee. We would grow old together and be best friends for life. And now she was moving to the other side of the country! This was not how things were supposed to go.

Resentment swelled in me. I had to hang up before I told her how I really felt.

That night as I scraped my uneaten dinner into the garbage disposal, I listened to my parents talking enthusiastically about Kelly's good fortune. They weren't fooling me. I knew their hearts were broken too.

In my mind I couldn't erase the picture of Kelly and me giggling in our playhouse made out of an old refrigerator box. She was eight and I was five. Inside, using brightly colored chalk, we had drawn windows complete with shades and frilly green curtains.

Daydreaming out our make-believe windows, my sister and I had conjured up a whole grown-up world that the two of us would live in. Kelly was going to marry Donny Osmond. Greg from *The Brady Bunch* was more my style.

And every night we would end our bedtime prayers with a spit and a handshake reaffirming our deal. God would keep us together forever.

I knew growing up wouldn't be exactly as we'd planned. She was soon to be married; I was just out of college and still living with Mom and Dad. But whatever the future might bring, I at least thought I would have my sister by my side.

Mom gingerly tapped me on the shoulder. "Sharon, we have to talk." I'll say! Finally, someone understood my side of all this.

"Sharon," she said, "as the maid of honor you have to plan a wedding shower for Kelly before she leaves."

With all the sarcasm I could muster, I said, "Let me make sure I understand this. Kelly is ditching me and now I have to throw her a party? Do I have this straight?"

As I looked to my mother for a reply, I saw that her expression was wistful.

"I'm not happy about Kelly leaving either," she said. "But we have to do this for her, no matter how hard it is. Remember the verse I always used to read to you and Kelly? 'So faith, hope, love abide, these three; but the greatest of these is love.' Those are the words we have to focus on now."

With a gleam of determination in her eyes, Mom got down to business. She whipped out a list entitled "Things to Do," and proceeded to outline a master plan.

For the next three weeks, my mother and I were a finely tuned shower-planning machine—but with different motivations. Mom was working toward creating a day that would live forever in Kelly's memory. I saw planning the shower as an opportunity to avoid the pain of facing my sister.

Whenever Kelly called, I came up with an excuse not to talk to her. The evening I was supposed to help Kelly pack, I conveniently had other plans. When my mother asked why I'd let my sister down, I said, "I couldn't tell Kelly I was getting ready for her surprise wedding shower, could I?" I consoled myself with the notion that after the shower, Kelly would understand why I'd been "busy." But I wasn't kidding anyone, least of all myself.

Before we knew it, the day of the shower was upon us. When the guests arrived, they all mingled politely. I sat in a corner alone.

I heard my mother telling about Kelly and Roger's delightful future. "They'll be finding a place to live soon, and the climate out there is ideal. . . ." I rolled my eyes and groaned.

Suddenly someone called out, "She's here!"

Thirty women stampeded to their seats. Within seconds, the lights were out and cameras at the ready. We heard Kelly trudging up the porch steps, her car keys jangling.

"Surprise!"

Kelly was in a daze as everyone whirled around her with hugs and kisses. Mom worked her way through the crowd to pin a corsage on my sister's blouse. As Kelly wiped away my mother's tears, she said, "Oh, Mommy, I—"

My mother gently put her finger over Kelly's lips. "You're welcome," she said.

After lunch Kelly opened her gifts. I went to get the coffee and dessert.

Over the gurgling percolator I could hear the guests laughing and applauding. But I just couldn't go out there. I managed to keep bustling and flitting about enough that I missed the entire shower. But from what I could tell in the kitchen, all had gone well. As my mother escorted the last of the guests outside, I finally gathered the courage to look in the living room.

Kelly was sitting in the chair we'd decorated with ribbons and a pink parasol. Someone had made a hat by covering a paper plate with bows from her gifts. I watched as Kelly tied it under her chin. And in that instant, a memory came back to me.

She and I were playing wedding in the new spring grass. She was dressed as a bride in Mom's old white curtains, and her blond hair shimmered in the sun. In her hand was a bouquet of dandelions I'd picked. I was toddling along behind, fluffing her train as she marched barefoot up an aisle made of beach towels.

My eyes misted at the memory and I reached up to brush away the wetness. When I dropped my hand, Kelly was standing directly in front of me. I looked into her eyes. My sweet childhood sister was there. But now so was a glorious grown-up woman. A woman with a life of her own.

"I'm so sorry I avoided you, Kelly. I felt scared that you were going away. I didn't want things to change. I figured if I were mad at you, saying goodbye wouldn't hurt so much . . ."

"Since when do we have to tell each other we're sorry? Besides, we have a deal, remember?"

Kelly spat in her palm and shook my hand. We both burst out laughing and hugged. I buried my face in her shoulder. I wanted to remember everything about this moment.

"Sharon, our deal isn't about miles. It's better than that now. It's about remembering the love in our hearts for each other, no matter where we are."

She was right. The closeness I had been afraid would slip away now felt stronger than I could have ever imagined. I wasn't afraid of losing her anymore.

So the greatest of these is love. Sounded like a good deal to me.

There was absolutely no time when I didn't love her.

HER HEART ON HER SLEEVE

ROSEMARY CLOONEY

In all the comings and goings of those years in Maysville, my sister was the one constant. I was six years older than [my brother] Nicky, and we became real friends later. But I was just three when Betty was born, so we grew up together. There was hardly ever a time when I didn't share a room with her, play with her, laugh and talk and fight with her. And there was absolutely no time when I didn't love her.

Betty always listened to me, always did what I said we'd do. One very cold winter day, when I was five and Betty just about two, we got dressed up in two of our aunt's long dresses. "Now we have to go down to the river," I told Betty, "because we're going on a long trip, and we have to wait by the river till the boat comes."

Somehow we managed to sneak down the stairs and out of the house without being seen. We scurried across Front Street, clutching the folds of our long gowns. We were standing at the edge of the river grading, and I was looking upriver, pretending I could just see the boat coming, when Betty skidded down the slick grading into the river. The dark water closed above her head.

I leaned over, grabbed her hand, and dragged her out. She wasn't crying, just coughing and sputtering. I got her home and into the bathtub and then dried off, all by myself.

My mother had told me I would manage, I would be able to do whatever had to be done. Betty and I formed a bond, very early, that I was sure nothing would ever break. "We'll always be together," I promised her one day, when we'd just been moved from one place to another. "I'll never leave you behind." I felt absolutely certain nobody else would ever come between us, and I was right. Nobody else did. . . .

⌇⌇⌇

Betty was only ten when we moved, but already sure of herself in a way I could only admire, but never expect to achieve. When a kid down the block began bullying Nicky, and Nicky told Betty and me, my sister took action.

Betty marched down the block, Nicky and I trailing, and found the kid sitting on his porch steps. "You've been beating up my brother," she said fiercely, making a fist. The kid looked at this knobby-kneed, skinny little girl and laughed. Betty's fist shot out and clipped him alongside his ear. The boy ran into his house, howling.

That evening his parents pounded on our door. "Your granddaughter beat up our son," they informed Grandma. "We expect an apology."

Again, Nicky and I trailed along. Betty walked briskly up the steps, not a moment's hesitation, and knocked. Instantly the door was yanked open. The boy's mother loomed in the doorway, arms folded, glaring; her husband was a frowning figure behind her.

Betty regarded them for a moment, then folded her arms and turned to Nicky and me. "My, my," she said brightly. "Look what we have here! A reception committee!" . . .

Movies were our gateway to a boundless world. The screen glowed with the possibilities we'd always known must be out there—people to see, places to go—around the bend in the river. At night in our attic bedroom, three narrow cots in a row, scrunched under Grandma's worn warm quilts, we'd review the movie we'd just seen, quoting dialogue, planning trips we'd take together. To Singapore, after seeing Sydney

Greenstreet under the ceiling fans at Raffles. To Venice on the Orient Express. To magical marvelous places. No matter where we went, we'd go together. . . .

Sixes

The farther I got from most of my family, the closer I felt to Betty and the closer Betty felt to almost everybody. More than ever, she wore her heart on her sleeve, and it was a heart as big as all outdoors—or at least as big as the band bus. She lavished warmth on everyone: the bus driver, Uncle George, the waitresses in the all-night diners. I teased her about how often she said, "I love you." One night in a hotel, she glanced at me. "Listen to this" she said as she picked up the phone to leave a wake-up call. "Goodnight, operator," she said, winking at me. "I love you."

A New
Sisterhood

A love of a longtime friend creates a new sisterhood.

TWICE BLESSED

RITA NONEMAN BAUGHMAN

nn and I grew up right down the block from each other in the small town of Paulding, Ohio, near the Indiana state line. Our mothers were sisters, and it felt like Ann and I were too. We were almost inseparable, up till all hours giggling and telling stories, walking to school and the library, and shopping downtown. We even double-dated to our junior/senior prom.

"We'll be friends for life, won't we?" Ann said that night.

"Always," I agreed.

We both married and began raising families of our own. Ann moved across the Indiana line to Fort Wayne, and I made my home in Austin, Texas. There were too many miles between us for the kind of closeness we'd known before. Still, over the years, we talked on the phone, sharing everything as always. Once she called me with disturbing news. "I have PKD," she said. I knew what the initials meant: polycystic kidney disease. Ann's family had a history of PKD. It had claimed the lives of her father and grandfather and left Ann with malfunctioning kidneys. The kidneys filter waste fluids and regulate vital substances in the body. When they lose their function, toxins build up in the blood. I knew Ann would someday need a new kidney, and I offered her one of mine. In 1998 her doctor said a transplant was essential.

"Do you remember what I once told you?" I asked.

"Yes," Ann said, "but I can't let you do it."

"No arguments," I said. "If I'm a match, I want to be your donor."

Other members of Ann's family were considered unsuitable because of their medical history. I didn't hesitate to be tested. My sons were afraid for me, but I wasn't. There are risks involved in giving up a kidney. The surgery, though, is relatively simple. And often the donor's remaining kidney grows and functions at greater capacity.

For the next six months, I went through screening. My blood type matched Ann's, and I was declared healthy. I waited in Austin for the call. Finally in May 1999, a date was set and we were assigned rooms at University Hospital in Indianapolis, close to home for Ann and one of the best transplant hospitals in the country.

The day before the operation I convinced Ann to go shopping. "Well, we need decent pajamas, don't we?" I said.

It seemed like old times, the two of us shopping together before a sleepover. But when I looked at Ann walking slowly ahead of me, I was startled to see how weak she was, how much she'd changed. God, I prayed, make this work. Please make Ann healthy again.

Both Ann and I had more tests right before surgery to be sure we were up to it. The doctors focused on my well-being every bit as much as Ann's, and I had all confidence in the surgeon who would perform the operation.

The next day, after it was over, I felt weak, but had expected as much. I got out of bed and put on the new robe Ann and I had bought together. I couldn't wait to check on her down the hall.

"Morning, sunshine," I said, peeking into her room.

"We did it, didn't we," Ann said. She pulled back the covers on her bed and patted the space beside her. I crawled in next to her, and we giggled and talked like we were kids again.

Everything seemed perfect, and in two days I made preparations to go back home. My sons had already kissed me good-bye and were on a plane for Austin. I sat down to make a list of thank-yous I wanted to write, but I had trouble holding the pen. I had no strength in my right arm. For the first time in this whole experience, I was afraid. I buzzed for a nurse.

Just when I thought I'd had every test in the book, I had another. The surgeon ordered an MRI, and it revealed something that had lain secret for years. "You have a benign tumor on your brain," the doctor said, "and it has to be removed. You're in good hands here with us, Rita, and I'd like to schedule the operation right away. Okay?"

I nodded. I can deal with this. I called my boys in Texas. They repacked their bags and got on a plane back to Indianapolis. I went back to Ann's room and told her the news. "I'll be with you every step of the way," she said, putting her arm around me. "You should have known this earlier, Rita. You never should have gone ahead with the transplant."

"No, no," I said. "You don't understand. I was meant to help you first."

To build my strength, I began walking the hospital halls in preparation for another surgery. I'd remained on the transplant wing, and I glanced into the patients' rooms as I passed. Everyone here was either a giver or receiver of the gift of life. God's angels were everywhere.

The day of the operation, exactly a week after the transplant surgery, I found myself with more than twenty family members and friends surrounding me. Ann, already the picture of health, stood beside my gurney holding my hand—and she was there by my bed when I awoke after surgery. "You're fine," she said. "Everything went well." Yes, everything, I thought. It happened in exactly the sequence God wanted it to happen. I'd saved a life, and then my own was saved.

"I'm so lucky to have you," Ann whispered.

"We have each other," I said. We were friends for life. Twice blessed.

*I often stop to marvel at our closeness,
and I wish I could thank my father.*

MY FATHER'S GIFT

JO COUDERT

As the only child of young parents, I grew up in a warm, close threesome. When I was small, in the days before seat belts, I rode standing between my mother and father in the car, a hand on each of their shoulders. I sat between them at dinner and breakfast, went picnicking and camping with them, and when they went out in the evening, slept on any handy bed until it was time to be picked up and carried home again. I never doubted my place in the family, and it wouldn't have occurred to me to wish for a sister or brother to share it.

That came later, when I was seventeen and my parents' marriage took a wrong turn. Then I longed to have a sibling to divide the terrible burden of being in the middle: "Tell your father . . ." "Tell your mother . . ." I was still a child, after all, so it was no surprise that my peacemaking attempts failed. The quarrels escalated, and one day my father left.

After the divorce, my mother moved to Florida, and I found work and a place to live in the city. My father, someone told me, had married again, to a girl only slightly older than I. It would have been easy for him to find me, and I believed he would come when time had healed the wounds. But finally I gave up hoping and accepted that I was never going to see or hear from him again.

Fast-forward twenty-odd years. My photograph appeared in ads for a book I had written, and in the mail one day came a letter. The return address had the initial C and the same last name as mine. A cousin writing to compare branches of the family tree, I thought, until I read the pulse-stopping first sentence. "I don't know if you know about me," it read, "but I'm your sister."

My sister? Nonsense. I was an only child. Well, perhaps there were two daughters from my father's second marriage, as this Carolyn was claiming, but my father was dead, and what had these sisters to do with me?

But I was forced to admit to myself that Carolyn did sound nice. She was in her first job, teaching high school English. She had hopes of becoming a writer too. She imagined, judging from my photo, that there was a family resemblance. Curiosity got the better of me. I invited her to dinner.

On the appointed evening, I opened the door to a person of my height and body build, with the same deep brown eyes and high forehead. "Goodness," I exclaimed without thinking, "we look enough alike to be sisters." We both laughed. I drew her inside, and we began to talk.

It was quickly apparent that we had much more than looks in common. We were both readers, both lovers of the theater and ideas. I found I liked this person.

My overwhelming feeling was amazement, but Carolyn's was contentment. She described herself as the odd person out in a family with a remote father who had died when she was young and an extroverted mother and sister who cared about sports, business and practical matters. When, at fifteen, she learned of my existence, she wove a fantasy of a sister who would see life as she did, tell her its secrets, be her companion.

How often do dreams come true? Rarely, but this one has. Time went by and we became friends. As we got to know each other, an instinctive sympathy and special understanding grew between us. Maybe we are lucky that we were never rivals for our parents' attention, never had to share a room or toys or clothes, never teased each other or built up resentments. But I like to think it is the mysterious tie of sisterhood that has led to our deep and abiding affection.

Carolyn has what she wanted—someone like her to talk to. And I have something I never knew was missing from my life—a sister. We are there for each other, getting together as often as our separate lives allow. It is she who lives in the city now and I in the country; and after she has been to visit me or I have met her in the city for dinner and the theater, I often stop to marvel at our closeness, and I wish I could thank my father. It doesn't matter now that he never came. He sent me the gift of a sister instead.

She turned out to be my mother's last and greatest gift to me.

FINDING MY SISTER

DOTTY WOODY

went to see my mom in northern California for what I thought would be the last time on a gray, rainy fall evening. I shielded my face from the downpour as I walked from my car to the house, feeling as though the sky itself were falling on me. Mom, a diabetic, was in such bad shape her doctors feared serious complications during her upcoming angioplasty operation.

In Mom's room, I set the flowers I'd brought on her bedside table, wishing I could have brought her what she really wanted. I've failed her, I thought, as I sat beside her bed and held her hand, the hand where she wore the ring with the birthstones of each of her children. Three gems on the left and three on the right symbolized me and my five brothers and sisters. But the setting in the middle was empty.

I was twelve years old when Mom first told me about my long-lost sister. I had just set down my books after getting home from school one spring afternoon. When I went to the kitchen to get a snack, I saw Mom wiping away tears with her apron. "Mom, why are you crying?" I'd asked.

"I guess you're old enough to understand now," she said. "You know how much I love you and your brothers and sisters, don't you?"

I nodded. I loved her so much I couldn't bear to see her cry.

"Well, when I was just a little older than you—fifteen—I had a baby girl I didn't get to watch grow up. I had to give her up for adoption. Today is her birthday. She's twenty-two."

Mom explained how she had met and married my father not long after giving up her baby. The baby's father had been killed in a car accident. Mom never knew what became of the daughter she had given away. "Her birthday's when I miss her most," Mom said. "I wish I knew how her life has been—if she forgives me for letting her go." She covered her face with her hand and my eyes fell on the ring with the multicolored birthstones that I loved to see glitter in the sunlight. So that's why the middle stone's missing, I thought. That's why Mom always gets so sad when I ask her about it. I knew the birthstone for April was a diamond and I imagined how perfect it would look in the center of her ring.

I drew her hand away from her face and hugged her. Somewhere I had another sister. What did she look like? Did she ever wonder about Mom? I knew how much Mom missed me even the hours I was at school each day. How it must hurt her to have never seen her first daughter again.

As the years went by, I asked Mom lots of questions about her first baby. I learned the hospital where she was born, the name of the adoption agency that placed her, the color of her eyes. At first I was driven by the wish to know more about this lost piece of Mom's life—of our life—this person she loved as much as I loved her. More than anything else I was curious. Gradually a resolution grew inside me. I wanted to find my half sister.

When Mom was diagnosed with diabetes, my plan took on a new urgency. In 1990, the day I turned eighteen, I told Mom, "I'm going to find her for you. Then your ring will finally be complete."

I started at the adoption agency, but they could tell me little because of confidentiality laws. I contacted all kinds of social service agencies, hoping to find some record of the baby. I even called a private investigator. He offered me my first real hope of locating my sister, but the two-thousand-dollar fee he wanted was out of the question. I had just gotten out of high school and could barely afford bus fare.

So it was back to square one. I kept writing, kept calling, kept checking, and each April 8 when my sister's birthday rolled around, I'd renew my promise to my mother. Time and again I met with dead ends. It felt as if I was searching for a diamond on a beach. Mom's daughter had been adopted somewhere not far from where Mom still lived, but that was more than thirty years ago. She could be anywhere by now.

In 1996, Mom's health took a sharp turn for the worse. By October, when I visited her before the angioplasty, I had to face the fact that time had run out. The next day I had to go back to North Carolina. But sitting beside Mom in her hospital room, the life I had there suddenly felt empty. I'm too young to lose her, I thought. And then I thought of my half sister, the daughter who didn't even know the precious mother she was losing.

"I'm sorry, Mom," I said. "I wish I could have found her. I really wanted to."

"You've done all you could, honey," Mama said to me. But I still despaired that I couldn't keep this one promise to her.

I called every day from North Carolina, hearing Mom's voice get weaker each time. The day of the operation, I kept wishing I had found her first daughter so she could be praying for Mom too. Finally the phone rang. I answered it and heard the sweetest sound ever: my mother's voice.

"You're okay!" I said.

"Honey, it's a miracle. They told me I died on the operating table and came back."

"Mom!"

"I want to tell you about the incredible vision I had," she said. "I saw a tall, handsome man. He was glowing with white light. I told him I was ready to go with him, that I didn't want any more pain. But he said no, he couldn't take me. He said I had unfinished business. Next thing I knew I was awake again."

Mom assumed the "unfinished business" was looking out for me, since I was living so far from home. But to me the meaning of Mom's vision was clear. This is a second chance to reunite her with her first child, I thought. I have to keep looking.

The breakthrough I was hoping for came shortly after, when I learned about the internet. I got access to a computer, and the very first time I went online, a new world of possibilities opened up. I posted messages on bulletin boards asking for advice and help on searching for my half sister. Just two days later, I got a reply from Susan Friel-Williams, of an Internet search agency called BigHugs.com. "I'm already doing a search in the year of your sister's birth for another client, so I can search for her at no cost to you," she wrote. "I feel like I'm meant to help you." Later that week was Thanksgiving Day. Thank you, God, I prayed, for sending Mom back to us. Please help me keep my promise to her.

Two days after, Susan sent me contact information for someone she thought was a relative of my lost sister. Without hesitation I picked up the phone and called him, asking him to pass on my number.

But when I hung up, doubts flooded my mind. What if she thought we were cranks? Or if she didn't want to speak to us? What if she was angry or just didn't care? An anxious tug-of-war went on inside me. What if after all this, she never calls?

The next day, the first of December, dawned drizzly and cold. I dusted and vacuumed, trying not to think too much. Early that afternoon the phone rang. I grabbed it. "Hello?"

"Hi, this is Candi. Candi Johnson." A pause. "I was told I might be your sister."

I let out my breath in a long sigh. "Oh, I'm so glad you called!"

At first I had to ease her doubts, explain how I found her, how I knew Mom was indeed her birth mother. But soon we were talking as if we called each other every day. Amazingly, we discovered we had lived only twenty miles apart in

California at one point. And now, here we were both living in the South. Candi had moved to Virginia when she'd married her husband, an Air Force officer. "I used to wonder if my birth mother ever thought about me," Candi told me.

"Every year on your birthday, she cries," I told her.

There was silence for a moment. "I know how hard it must have been for her to give me up," Candi said. "I've always wanted to tell her how happy I am, that I'm so grateful to her."

As soon as we hung up, I called Mom and gave her Candi's phone number.

When I talked to Mom again her voice sounded stronger than I'd heard it in a long while. "I can't believe I just spoke to my baby," she kept saying. It was what I'd hoped for since Mom had first told me about my long-lost sister all those years before.

Mom and Candi arranged to meet and we all looked forward to the family reunion. But before it could take place, Mom passed away on January 22, 1997. She never saw her oldest daughter, but I knew Mom had left this world in peace.

In April, I went to visit Candi. As soon as I laid eyes on her, I gasped, "You look just like Mom!" There were so many resemblances—the way she walked, the way she smiled, even the way she whistled through her teeth. We sat down and I opened Mom's jewelry box.

I showed Candi various necklaces and bracelets, explaining the significance of each, then took out the birthstone ring Mom had always worn. "She kept the center spot open for you," I said. "Now we can finally put in the diamond that belongs there." When Candi wore the ring the next morning to church, it was like having Mom right there with us.

Candi met my other siblings and then I met her adoptive parents. Digging into mounds of spaghetti amid the laughter and jokes at the dinner table, I thought of similar evenings with Mom in her apron, ladling sauce onto our heaping plates.

The more Candi and I talked, the closer we grew. Our goals, our personalities, our whole approach to life are so similar, it's uncanny. Today, Candi is my best friend. We're constantly running up the phone bill and e-mailing each other.

I had wanted to find my half sister as a gift to my mom. But Candi has turned out to be my mother's last and greatest gift to me, a comfort after losing her so early. Now whenever I look at Mom's birthstone ring, I think of how God's angels—heavenly and human—helped make all our lives complete.

*The sweet and slippery word "sister" embraces
real sisters and all the sisterhoods in between.*

SISTERS AND SECRETS

LETTY COTTIN POGREBIN

"Have you any brothers or sisters?"

It's a question I dread, yet people ask it all the time. At best, it's a caring question on the road to intimacy. We want to know more about one another's origins, to understand who we are and where we come from. At worst, it's fueled by conversational drought: "Where'd you grow up?" we ask when we run out of things to say. "Got any sisters or brothers?"

To most people, the answer is simple. "I'm one of four girls," they reply. "I have two brothers." "I'm an only child."

But when I get the question, I have to make a split-second decision. Do I finesse it and just say "I have two sisters," or do I take several minutes of my listeners' time, test their powers of concentration, and tell them the whole story? Sisterhood is such a complicated subject for me: it's about biology and family history, lies and love, identity, secrecy, and the gut-level truth that one distills not from facts, but from feelings. Most of all, for me, sisterhood is about equality and acceptance. No other definition can contain my convoluted story.

I have two sisters but only one of them feels like a sister—Betty, who is fourteen years older than I. She's the sister who lived at home until the morning of her wedding; she left when she was twenty-one and I was seven. She's the sister who taught me how to tell time, the sister who set her hair in bobby pins and combed it in a pageboy, the sister who dated handsome boys in uniform and wore leg makeup during World War II when stockings were rationed, the person I've always called my sister and thought of as my sister—my real sister, my only sister—even though I discovered when I was twelve that she was born of a different father and was in fact my half sister, whom my father adopted after he abandoned his own daughter, who was also my half sister but whom I never met until I was almost fifteen years old and she twenty-seven.

Are you with me? Let's try again.

By blood, I'm related equally to both of my sisters: Betty, born in 1925, is my mother's daughter by her first marriage. Rena, born in 1927, is my father's daughter by his first marriage. For years, my parents concealed their previous unions from me and most of their friends. The relatives cooperated in the ruse. Much later, when a cousin spilled the beans and my parents had to answer for their lies, they explained that when they were young, divorce was considered a scandal, a personal, if not moral, failure, especially for a woman. So, like thousands of others trapped in the mores of the time, they created a cover-up. After they married each other in 1937 and I was born in 1939, they moved to a new place and seized the opportunity to erase their prior lives and invent a more respectable family history. Their divorces vanished into thin air. The rough edges of their biographies were filed as smooth as a well-honed myth. They backdated their wedding to 1923 to accommodate Betty's birth date. My father legally adopted Betty and at the same time became estranged from his own daughter, Rena. With a fresh slate, my parents could present themselves to their new community as a long-married couple with two daughters, Betty and me, her baby sister—a love child born to this long-married pair "after fourteen years of trying." In short, a normal, all-American family.

From the perspective of my early childhood, our family seemed not just normal but enviable. I had this wonderful big sister who treated me like a living doll, adored me, indulged me, and then, when taking leave of her parents' home, made me the flower girl at her wedding. What more could a seven-year-old want? A kid doesn't question her family mythology. I never noticed that our family albums contained no pictures of my parents' wedding or that none of the photos showed Daddy and Betty in the same shot until she was fourteen. I was too busy lingering over the images I loved, like the one of Betty and me on the back porch in our summer outfits, she a fully developed young woman, and me a pudgy toddler imitating her grown-up pose; or dressed for a costume party, she looking sexy in an army cap and boots, and me in a grass skirt.

My memories of our time together are sparse but precious. I remember being the much-fussed-over mascot at her slumber parties in our finished basement, with her friends in their satin pajamas lounging on mounds of pillows, trying on lipstick, playing 78 rpm records, and talking about boys. It was Betty who taught me to eat spaghetti with butter and ketchup; hold the sauce. It was she who started me listening to "our" favorite radio shows—*Burns and Allen, The Easy Aces, Mr. Keen: Tracer of Lost Persons*—and keeping track of the top tunes on *Martin Bloch's Make-Believe Ballroom*. And thanks to her, I learned all the words to "Mares Eat Oats" and "Comin' in on a Wing and a Prayer" and "White Cliffs of Dover"—wartime melodies that somehow belong to my childhood as much as to her dating years.

Best of all, I remember our trip to a fabric store when she was engaged and shopping for her new life. The salesman mistook me for her daughter. "No, we're sisters!" Betty laughed, reaching down to hug my little-girl shoulders. "We're sisters!" I beamed, the fourteen years between us melting away as I basked in the status of an equal.

The day after Betty's wedding, my parents moved me into her room with its tiny rosebud wallpaper and mirrored dressing table swathed in an organdy skirt. I was thrilled, but I missed her terribly. Looking back, I suppose I might have preferred to have had a sister who was a contemporary, someone with whom I could play paper dolls and ring-a-levio, rather than a glamorous college girl living in a different world under the same roof. And with each passing year, as my parents' marriage became a battleground, I might have wished for a sister to huddle with at the top of the stairs when their arguments shook the house and I alone absorbed the bickering, the shouting and sobbing, the weeks of turgid silence.

The truth is, I don't remember ever wanting any other sister. Though Betty was years older and miles away, I cherished her for everything she was and everything she brought into my life, especially for giving me a brother-in-law—no other kid my age had one—for making me an aunt when I was nine, and for having four terrific babies before she turned thirty, thus fulfilling every female fantasy of the 1950s to the letter. I loved her husband, Bernie, who was the spitting image of the actor Glenn Ford and the most dashing of all her uniformed suitors, a man of gentle wisdom who always made me feel as if I'd invented sunshine. I loved their kids—to me, the cutest, smartest, most lovable children on earth. I visited often, dropping into their *Good Housekeeping* life as if into a dream, all the while studying my sister's world like a painting foreground, background, light and shadow.

I watched her hang curtains, file recipes, tend a garden, make a budget and stick to it, use a pressure cooker and other newfangled appliances we'd never had at home. I studied how she organized the family chores, packed a picnic, cut the children's hair, gave them pots and pans to play with in the tub instead of bath toys, traced the family's vacation route on a map in Magic Marker so everyone could savor the trip before they left and relive it after they were home. I watched her and Bernie together. I memorized their pleasure. I unloaded my despair about Mommy and Daddy's fights, and my anxiety that they might split up. When they were fighting downstairs, I called Betty from the upstairs phone. "They're at it again!" I would cry, and Betty would comfort and reassure me, even help me to laugh at their quarrels, as if my parents were naughty children and I the adult forced to tolerate their misbehavior. And when I needed some joyful noise to drown out my father's roar and my mother's tears, I called up memories of Betty's family dinnertimes or the ruckus of her children's laughter. Because I had witnessed my sister's life I knew there was a better way.

I resolved to be exactly like her when my time came except I wouldn't have four children, I'd have five.

Then Rena showed up. I had learned of her existence only three years earlier when the revelation of our family secret had literally knocked me unconscious and I'd awakened to my parents' guilty excuses and explanations. But it was one thing to know I had another sister out there somewhere in the world, and quite another to answer the bell one cold, crisp day and find her standing on the doorstep.

Rena, then twenty-seven, said she had come, reluctantly, because "our" father was a lawyer and she needed a court order, a marshal, some kind of legal help to get her belongings out of her mother's house. The mother, my father's first wife, was deranged and violent. Rena said she could not stay with her another day.

After a reunion with our father that can only be described as sedate, and a dinner during which my mother seemed to be trying extra hard to make her feel welcome, Rena stayed with us for a while, helping to care for Mommy, who was ill with cancer. I rushed home from school every day to be with my newly discovered sister, as if she was a visiting mermaid who might disappear with the next wave. We talked constantly, or more accurately, she talked and I listened as magnificent sentences poured from her mouth, every one of them polysyllabic and professorial. She made obscure references to things like cybernetics, physiometry, and ethnographics. She corrected my mistakes. (Secrete means hide, not just ooze, and I've never forgotten it.) She sprinkled her arcane vocabulary into ordinary conversation and sent me rushing to the dictionary to look up words like "tautology" and "anima"—many of which I was tickled to encounter a few months later on the College Board exam.

Rena, it turns out, was a genius with an IQ of 180 and a Ph.D. in anthropology. She was the world's leading authority on Gypsy culture, a protégée of the great Ruth Benedict, and fluent in twenty Romani dialects. She'd been adopted by the Gypsy tribe that had been the subject of her doctoral thesis—by its king, no less, so she was a certified Gypsy princess. She wore Bohemian outfits and a thick long braid. She was exotic and eccentric.

She told me almost dispassionately how her mother heard voices and had hallucinations, and how she had beaten Rena mercilessly. Once the woman nearly blinded her with a blow to her eyes that broke her glasses. Several times her mother attempted to strangle her, and once she dangled her out of a window, bragging, "I gave birth to you, so I can kill you."

"Why did you stay?" I asked, incredulous.

Rena claimed she had nowhere else to go. She said she regretted having to turn to our father for help, but she had no choice.

"At this point, I'm interested in developing a compensatory relationship with you, not with him," she explained. "He could live without me all these years. I can live without him now."

"Daddy wanted to keep seeing you," I insisted, repeating the story my parents had told me when their lies caught up with them. "But he said your mother stopped the visits, poisoned you against him, and then threatened to harm you if he tried to get in touch or fight for you in court, so he stopped trying."

"My mother harmed me anyway," she said bitterly. "And he knew she would because she was always violent. No, that's not what happened." Rena insisted that his court-ordered visitation rights were contingent on his paying child support, and when he stopped paying, her mother stopped the visits. Rena added: "He never fought for me. He didn't want me. He left me alone with her, and I never heard from him again."

Suddenly, a huge, hot thought seared into a corner of my brain: If our father could abandon one daughter, he could abandon another. We're both his blood. Obviously, blood is no protection. Neither is time. She'd been with him twelve years; I was going on fifteen. I'm not safe. He could leave me too.

Then I thought of Rena, growing up without a daddy. My heart hurt for her. I must have seemed like her replacement, her father's new toy. Still, she had come back. She treated our father with icy propriety but she had forgiven me, the baby who started it all, and she had forgiven my mother. In fact, as Mommy's cancer worsened, Rena's kindness was one of her most endearing traits. She was helpful and solicitous in the manner of someone who had a lot of experience putting herself last.

She stayed over at our house for days at a time. Neighbors began to notice. Friends asked questions. Daddy told Rena he wanted to acknowledge her in the community, but rather than disentangle all of our complicated relationships at this late date, he asked if she would mind being introduced as a cousin.

To be disowned not once but twice, to be rejected after being rediscovered, to find her father more interested in the judgment of his community than the feelings of his daughter—how that must have stung. But Rena just nodded and said "cousin" was fine.

Soon afterward, she moved into her own apartment. I worked at our relationship, determined to make Rena a "real" sister like Betty. I marveled at her ways. She kept her entire wardrobe piled up on her ironing board and dressed herself from there. She wore sandals and dirndl skirts in an age of white gloves and matching shoes and bags. She was fascinating, intense, and utterly unique. As she revealed more and more about herself, I began to feel like an apprentice rather than a sister, especially when she took me to visit the Gypsies who'd adopted her. The tribe lived in a stretch of second-floor storefronts in upper Manhattan, but the king, a big man with a heavy black mustache, was right out of central casting. Most of the Gypsy women wore dozens of gold bracelets on both their arms; Rena told me they didn't trust the banks so they converted their life's savings into gold bangles and wore them day and night. I remember the evening meal, when everyone ate directly from the serving platters. I remember, too, how well they treated their children—like miraculous treasures. It was hard to know which child belonged to which parent because each was showered with love and attention by everyone. And I remember how the Gypsies adored their princess—Rena, my sister.

As did I. My adolescent crush, a fevered outburst of interest and affection expressed itself in paroxysms of imitation. I wore sandals and black turtlenecks. I determined that I would become an intellectual. I would live alone. I might not ever marry. I believed I was a more interesting person just for having Rena as my sister. Meanwhile, Betty's life, happy as it was, suddenly seemed tepid, colorless, and conventional by comparison.

When I was fifteen—three days before Betty's thirtieth birthday—our mother died. That summer, I moved in with Betty and Bernie. I drove their car. I had no curfew. I went my own way. In the full flush of my grief, my teen rebellion, my awestruck adoration of Rena, my dumb risk-taking, my acting-out, Betty remained my most ardent booster. When I confided my inadequacies—small breasts, skinny ankles, mousy hair—she listened, took me seriously, then proceeded to counter my claims in her no-nonsense, English-teacher voice, with the tenderness just below the surface, building my confidence and reiterating my strengths until I felt like Marie Curie and Debbie Reynolds rolled into one. Somehow, she gave me unconditional love and firm guidance without becoming my parent or disciplinarian.

How she communicated this fundamental regard for me, I really don't know. She just put it into the air we breathed—a sense of rock-solid sisterness, a respect for boundaries, an utter absence of condescension regardless of the disparities in our age, interests, development, and personal style. Somehow, she made me feel we were peers, and with that feeling, I was able to go off to college that autumn a surer, stronger person. . . .

The infatuation with Rena showed cracks after I graduated from college and started to see myself as a serious person with thoughts and ideas of my own. Though I still admired her greatly, I was ready to relate to her on more even ground while she seemed unable to approach me without the patronizing tone of a lecturing professor. The remarkable mutuality and respect that Betty had shown me throughout my childhood seemed out of Rena's ken though she was "only" twelve years my senior, not fourteen. The breach widened even more when she married a man who seemed so wrong for her that it was hard to square my remarkable Rena with her choice of mate, and harder still to spend time with them.

We drifted apart. She had two children, wrote books and articles, and taught at a college in New York. I got married, had three children, wrote books and articles, and lived in New York. Having things in common could not compensate for the imbalances between us. It could not fill the gaps in our past or give her back the fourteen lost years with "our" father or relieve my vague sense of guilt. I always felt some complicity in causing Rena's suffering. What's more, I knew the family life I'd had and she'd coveted was far from the happy idyll she imagined. Still, she was the wronged one, the unacknowledged daughter, the secret sister who never quite fit in.

Over the years, Betty and I invited Rena to family gatherings but she almost always declined. Occasionally, she and I have lunch or exchange letters, but the wall between us has thickened with time. Today, to my regret, we are merely courteous acquaintances and I have resigned myself to the fact that I am a woman with two sisters—one who is cherished and close, and one whom I hardly know.

Having said that, I cannot pretend that the bond I have with Betty—wonderful as it is—is typical of other sisters. My twin daughters, now twenty-nine, have taught me what it means to enjoy bone-deep intimacy with another female and made me understand what Betty and I missed because of our age spread, generational differences, and separation over space and time. I've watched my daughters weave their lives together until they can read each other's thoughts, make each other laugh or cry, finish each other's sentences. Each knows the other thoroughly, historically, wordlessly, back to infancy and up to yesterday. Although both are married now, and each is a well-defined woman with a separate life, at some deep level, they have each other in a way Betty and I—for all our genuine love and equality—do not. Theirs is sisterhood of another sort, a sisterhood we could never have had.

Likewise, among my friends, I've seen sisters who talk every day and share the most minute details of their daily lives. It's a habit they fell into growing up and they've kept at it. Betty and I never overlapped in life long enough to develop such a routine. I rarely know what she's doing tomorrow and she generally doesn't know where I was last weekend. We don't go shopping together. We've never discussed sex. But we share the most important things—happiness, misery, family, politics, core values. From her, I still feel the same unconditional acceptance that sustained me in my troubled youth; and for her, I feel the same prideful love that I remember as a seven-year-old in the fabric store, beaming under my big sister's smile.

Writing this, I realize how sweet and slippery is this word "sister"—big enough to stretch beyond biology and across time; flexible enough to define soulmates and virtual strangers; precise enough to embrace me and Rena, me and Betty, my two daughters, and all the sisterhoods in between.

I couldn't imagine being happy while she was so sad.

STAR OF THE PAGEANT

ANN LYONS

I could barely sit still and eat at the dinner table that Christmas Eve in 1979. In just a couple of hours, I would play Mary in the Christmas pageant at church. The lights would shine down on me as I cradled the baby Jesus. The best part was that my family would all be in the audience—Mommy, Daddy, my three little sisters, and, of course, Terra.

Terra had become my foster sister two years earlier. My own sisters were much younger, so I was thrilled to have a playmate my own age. We spent hours in the warm Florida sunshine playing hopscotch and hide-and-seek. We traded secrets and giggled together. I felt like she'd always been part of our family.

I glanced over at her, seeking a reassuring smile to calm my nervousness about the performance. But she was staring down at her food; she'd eaten even less than me. Mom must have noticed her full plate too. "What's the matter, Terra?" she asked.

Terra looked up from her plate with brimming eyes. "Why didn't I get a part in the Christmas pageant?"

I drew in a startled breath. It was true—Terra didn't have a part in the play. I'd been so thrilled about my own role that I hadn't even thought about it.

Mommy put down her fork. "Well, honey, there aren't enough parts for everyone," she said. "It doesn't mean you're any less special."

But she should have a part, I thought. The rest of the meal was terribly quiet. I kept glancing over at Terra, who continued to pick listlessly at her food. Suddenly I couldn't imagine being in the play without her, being happy while she was so sad. I closed my eyes. I don't want Terra to feel left out. Please, God, make her see how special she is to us.

We finished dinner and set off for church. When we arrived and were piling out of the car, the director of the pageant saw us and came right over. "We've been waiting for you, Ann. Hurry and get into your costume." I hesitated, not wanting to leave Terra behind. Then the director turned to her. "And Terra. One of the actors is sick. Would you mind playing an angel tonight?" Terra stood there, not speaking, a smile slowly lighting up her face. I grabbed her hand and we ran inside to change.

The pageant began and I played my part, eagerly waiting for Terra's entrance. And then I saw her coming up the aisle, her face glowing brighter than all the church candles put together. She took her place behind the manger and lifted her shiny, white angel wings high above her head. There in her costume, with the light shining down on her, she was the star that night. But to me she was an angel every single day.

AUTHOR INDEX

TITLE INDEX

ACKNOWLEDGMENTS *(continued from page 4)*
GOODWIN, DORIS KEARNS. An excerpt from *Wait Till Next Year* by Doris Kearns Goodwin. Copyright © 1997 by Blithedale Productions. Used by permission of Simon & Schuster. GOULD, JOHN. "Praying for Mother to Stay" from *The Christian Science Monitor,* January 15, 1999. Used by permission of John Gould. GRUNWALD, LISA. "Sisters" from *Glamour,* July 1995. JAMES, SUSAN. "All I Ever Wanted" from *Country Living,* Nov. 1993. Used by permission of the author. JANSEN, DAN. "Jane" from *Full Circle* by Dan Jansen. Copyright © 1994 by the author. Used by permission of Villard Books, a division of Random House, Inc. JUDD, NAOMI. An excerpt from *Love Can Build a Bridge.* Copyright © 1993 by author Naomi Judd. Used by permission of Villard Books, a division of Random House, Inc. KING, CORETTA SCOTT. "Coretta and Edythe Scott" from *Sisters,* essays by Carol Saline. Copyright © 1994 by Carol Saline. Published by Running Press, PA. Used by permission of Writers House as agent for Coretta Scott King. KWAN, MICHELLE. "The Kwan Sisters" from *Heart of a Champion* by Michelle Kwan as told to Laura James. Copyright © 1997 by Michelle Kwan Corp. Reprinted by permission of Scholastic Inc. MANDRELL, BARBARA. "Get to the Heart" from *Get to the Heart: My Story* by Barbara Mandrell with George Vecsey. Copyright © 1990 by Barbara Mandrell. Used by permission of Doubleday Dell Publishing Group, Random House. NORRIS, KATHLEEN. "Borderline" from *The Cloister Walk.* Copyright © 1996 by author Kathleen Norris. Published by Riverhead Books, an imprint of Penguin Putnam Inc. Used by permission of the publisher. PARTON, DOLLY. "The Parton Sisters" from *Dolly: My Life and Other Unfinished Business.* Copyright © 1994 by Dolly Parton. Harper Collins Publishers. Used by permission of Dolly Parton Productions, Inc. PETERSON, BRENDA. "Sisters Stories" from *Sister Stories.* Copyright © 1996 by Brenda Peterson. Published by Viking, Penguin Group. Used by permission of the author. POGREBIN, LETTY COTTIN. "Sisters and Secrets" from *Sister to Sister,* edited by Patricia Foster, Anchor Books. Copyright © 1995 by Letty Cottin Pogrebin. Used by permission of Rosenstone/Wender. SCULLY, JULIA. "Lillian" from *Outside Passage: A Memoir of an Alaskan Childhood.* Copyright © 1998 by author Julia Scully. Used by permission of Random House, Inc. SIMONS, PAULLINA. "What Have You Done for Me Lately?" Copyright © 1999 by Paullina Simons. Used by permission of the author and The Joy Harris Literary Agency Inc. SPENCER, PAULA. "A Summer Storm" from *Woman's Day,* July 11, 2000. VAUTHIER, CRICKET HARDIN. "Animal Cracker Dresses." Used by permission of the author. VOLK, PATRICIA. "To My Sister" from *Redbook,* August 1995, The Hearst Corporation. WICKERSHAM, JOAN. "The Shadow of the Mountain" from *Sister to Sister,* edited by Patricia Foster, Anchor Books, 1995.

The following originally appeared in *Angels On Earth,* published by Guideposts, NY: "Twice Blessed" by Rita Noneman Baughman; "Down to Earth" by Colleen Hughes; "A Touch on the Shoulder" by Haven Webster; "Finding My Sister" by Dotty Woody. The following originally appeared in *Guideposts* Magazine: "Star of the Pageant" by Ann Lyons; "Sisters" by Martha Masters; "Sisters Pact" by Sharon Robertson; "The Unbreakable Bond" by Sharlene Sharpe and Darlene Goodson; "Sisters and Ladybugs" by Lauren Zylberman.

All possible care has been taken to fully acknowledge the ownership and use of the selections in this book. If any mistakes or omissions have occurred, they will be corrected in subsequent editions, provided notification is sent to the publisher.